THE UNIVERSITY OF MICHIGAN
CENTER FOR CHINESE STUDIES

MICHIGAN PAPERS IN CHINESE STUDIES
NO. 38

D1713442

VOICES FROM AFAR: MODERN CHINESE WRITERS
ON OPPRESSED PEOPLES AND THEIR LITERATURE

by
Irene Eber

Ann Arbor

Center for Chinese Studies
The University of Michigan

1980

Library of Congress Cataloging in Publication Data

Eber, Irene, 1929-
    Voices from afar.

    (Michigan Papers in Chinese Studies; no. 38)
    Includes bibliographical references and index.
    1. Chinese literature--Translations from foreign
languages--History and criticism. 2. Literature--
Translations into Chinese--History and criticism.
3. Discrimination in literature. I. Title.
II. Series.

PL2274.5.E2   809   80-10411
ISBN 0-89264-038-3

Printed in the United States of America

In memory of Ch'en Shou-yi

CONTENTS

ACKNOWLEDGEMENTS

In preparing this study I have benefited much from the encouragement of my friends at the University of Michigan, and I wish to thank them for the hours they have spent discussing this project with me. I am especially grateful for the many valuable suggestions made over the years by Harriet Mills and Norma Diamond.

To the Harvard-Yenching Library and its staff I owe a special debt of gratitude. In the course of many visits they unfailingly assisted me in the use of the library's holdings. To the staff of the Asia Library at the University of Michigan, and especially to Wan Wei-ying, I want to express my gratitude for the gracious and courteous help they gave me.

A post-doctoral Ford Foundation grant at the University of Michigan's Center for Chinese Studies in 1973-74 enabled me to complete research and begin writing. For the Center's generous financial and moral support I am grateful. The workshop and conference on "Modern Chinese Literature in the May Fourth Era" in 1974 offered the opportunity both for developing some of the themes of this study and for receiving much needed criticism. In 1975, the Nobel Symposium on "Modern Chinese Literature and its Social Context" once more allowed for the exploration of this topic and provided opportunities for invaluable discussions with Marian Galik and other European colleagues. I wish to offer my thanks to both for making my participation possible.

Portions of this manuscript were read by Naomi Hazan, Don Rimmington, and Ellis Tinios. I am most grateful for their valuable suggestions. Bonnie McDougall's suggestions after reading the complete manuscript are deeply appreciated. David Shulman, who gave the entire manuscript a painstaking reading must be thanked especially for his scrupulous care and attention to detail. Finally, I wish to thank Marlene Thom for her capable handling of editorial tasks.

x

The Kadoorie Family Fund for Chinese Studies—a project of the Fund for Higher Education (in Israel)—gave partial assistance for preparing the manuscript for publication.

PREFACE

The translation of literary works from one language and one cultural context into another poses questions common to both literary and intellectual history. Other people may learn of new literary techniques and subjects by means of translations or come in contact with new ideas and ways of thinking. The purpose of the present study is to understand the function of translations of Western literature in twentieth-century China, and to show how the translation of certain literary works was at specific times related to some major literary and intellectual currents. The translated literature will be considered from three aspects: how did Chinese commentators view the peoples whose writers wrote these literatures, what were their critical comments about the literary works, and what kinds of works were actually translated.

Four literatures were selected for study; the works of the Irish and the Poles, and works by Yiddish and black American authors. The Polish and Irish peoples are national entities with turbulent political histories. Jews and black Americans lived (and continue to live) as minorities within majority societies. All four considered themselves as having experienced a cultural and intellectual renaissance either in the nineteenth or the twentieth century, a renaissance that was expressed in increased literary creativity as well as in political and cultural life. In the 1920s especially, a number of Chinese writers and intellectuals took note of these renaissances and were impressed by the political and social problems raised in these literary works. In Chinese, Poles or Irish (in addition to others like Serbs, Hungarians, or Armenians) were referred to as small and weak (*jo-hsiao min-tsu*) or oppressed (*pei-ya-p'o min-tsu*) peoples. Their prose, poetry, and dramatic works were translated in considerable quantity throughout the twenties and thirties, and again in the fifties. Of the four literatures selected, examples from Polish are most numerous; those from black literature are much fewer.

xi

Translations from the literature of oppressed peoples were far fewer than translations from such major literatures as Russian or French. Similarly, Chinese literary criticism regarding the major literatures was more voluminous. But volume is not the significant consideration here; this literature was translated for a number of specific reasons. Whether as fiction, poetry, or drama, oppressed peoples' literature touched on practically all the major political and social issues that were discussed by Chinese intellectuals from the twenties to the fifties. Among these were the questions of nationalism and revolution, socialism and imperialism, social injustice, individual and class oppression, war, and improvement of the lot of the masses. Oppressed peoples' literature in their original languages was meant to be read by a broad audience, and for this reason its writers had been concerned with new uses of language and popular speech, as were also Chinese writers and intellectuals. The authors of this literature were patriotic men and women, individuals whose primary concern was the fate of their people as an entity and as a people with an identity. Such men and women, therefore, provided examples for those Chinese writers who also considered their literary activities as significant within a broader cultural and political context. In short, the literature of oppressed peoples confirmed for Chinese writers their own task and the role which they believed literature had in current change. In addition, from this literature Chinese readers could learn something about the world. But they could learn even more about themselves. Like the many fragmented images in a shattered mirror, oppressed peoples' literature projected the universal and multiple condition of oppression.

The subject of translating generally and translating the literature of oppressed peoples in particular raises a number of considerations. What factors within the literary scene will compel writers to translate, and how are their translations related to native literary production? What is the role of publishing and readership where works of translation are concerned? How can the works of strange and unknown peoples be translated and made plausible? How did a similarity of concerns, such as cultural oppression and renaissance, national identity and social inequality, influence Chinese critical evaluation of oppressed peoples' literature? How were experiments with literary techniques and new usages of language in this literature important to the goals of China's literary revolution in the twenties? How were ideological changes in Chinese literary and intellectual life reflected in both the choice of works to be translated and their critical evaluation?

I have tried to touch on these and related questions within the framework of intellectual and literary history. Little or no attention was therefore devoted to linguistic, artistic, or aesthetic considerations of the translated works. Although this admittedly neglects vital features of literature, I decided to pursue two major themes. One is that images of other peoples change in accordance with concepts unique to the people who create these images. The second theme is that translating as an intellectual activity is related to extra-literary factors. It is dependent on some prior or concurrent understanding (no matter how scanty or distorted) of the peoples who wrote the original works and it is stimulated by contemporary events and concerns of the translators' world.

Names have presented a problem throughout this study. Writers often signed articles and translations with their given names only or with various pennames. In most cases, neither surnames nor pennames could be traced. When a surname was known, I have supplied it in brackets. When an author was better known by his penname, like Mao Tun for example, I have used the penname in the text. Otherwise I have used the name with which the article or translation was signed, supplying whenever possible the actual name in parentheses. Translators and their pennames are listed in Appendix D.

INTRODUCTION

A primary consideration in the study of literary works in translation is that the original work written within its own cultural context and for a specific audience had a different function than the translated work produced within a new context and for a different audience. For originally written works there is a vast critical apparatus that examines how literature is created and which ends it serves. The subject of translations, however—"the re-enacting of someone else's creation," the motivation of translators, the choice of style and language, and the audience of translated works —is comparatively sparse. And yet, the translating of significant works of world literature has been with us for nearly as long as written records. Ever since humankind began to speak in different tongues, writes Störig, translating has been a necessary activity. Translating has been part of politics and social intercourse, war and commerce, and has played a role in the transmission of poetry, science, and philosophy. Indeed, "nearly all of intellectual history could be viewed and categorized in terms of important translating trends."[1] Translators are vital to any literature, writes Renato Poggioli; they are the cosmopolitans who assume the responsibility for disseminating a literary work. The number and quality of translators is significant in evaluating the strength and importance of a national literature.[2]

If we accept that translating is a valid activity and that its history is both long and illustrious, then why is there such a lack of critical tools? Why need we grope, probably unsuccessfully, for a clearer definition of what takes place when an original work moves from one context and language into another? No ready answers suggest themselves, primarily, I think, because translations are a many-sided phenomenon. We must recognize that not only is the original a work of art but that the skillful translation similarly has artistic merit; both the writer and translator are artists in their own right. Nonetheless, translation as an art form is unique because it is an interpretative art, and the product is both identical

with and different from the original. Much has been written on the
extent to which writers need be engaged in their world and the
degree to which a literary work is audience directed. To be sure,
a translator will often select a work he happens to know and like,
but there is little doubt that translations are to a great degree
audience directed. Translators must participate in the concerns
of their culture, and they must be able to assess whether a particular author or work will appeal to a readership. Moreover, a
translation may have an entirely different impact than the original
work. The question of impact is especially significant, but it is a
question that must be handled with extreme care, and it is necessary to differentiate between literary and extra-literary impact.
Shaw argues that translations can have a singular effect on both
areas. Translations from foreign literature can play a significant
role when a given literary tradition undergoes a radical change of
direction. Translations may then become part of political and social
movements, and "authors may seek in form or ideology that which
they can adapt or transmute for their own consciousness, time and
nation."[3] Shaw's assumptions are supported by Lowenthal's study
of the wide circulation of Dostoevsky's work in German translation
between 1880 and 1920. Lowenthal concludes that Dostoevsky in
German translation negatively influenced Germany's middle class in
developing the ability to champion and engage in social reform. His
analysis stresses the role of critics who created categories of inter-
pretation that were far more indicative of the ideology of their own
social groups than of Dostoevsky's works.[4]

Turning now from these wider considerations to China, there
is the question of the relationship between translated literature and
originally produced literary works. Most scholars agree that the
development of modern Chinese literature is indebted to translations
of foreign literature, especially of works from the nineteenth century. And it is a well-known fact that major authors from Japanese,
Russian, French, German, English, and American literature were
widely translated. However, it is not at all clear what kind of stimulus, for example, was provided by nineteenth-century Western
literature, and how this differed from the stimulus provided by
works from the twentieth century. It is also not clear how, precisely, the reception of nineteenth-century works differed from
that of twentieth-century works. Thus, lacking further a systematic survey of exactly which authors and which specific works were
translated from each century, an overall, clearly defined picture

of the relationship between translated and originally produced works does not appear.

As a group, the authors of modern Chinese literature command our attention, especially because the authors were in many cases also the translators. In creating new modes of literary expression they drew on traditional impulses and experience. Although the new writers were more cosmopolitan than any other generation before them, they were also steeped in Chinese traditional learning that they professed to reject at the same time. Therefore, the new literature they set out to create could not but be an outgrowth of Chinese literary tradition and its transformation, as well as the result of foreign stimuli.[5] These writers became more cosmopolitan as their environment changed, their outlook toward their own world and the world of others changing correspondingly. The emergence of modern Chinese literature, therefore, is also the result of writers developing new attitudes to a new reality. "They stress the intellectual value of literary works as a means of gaining a deeper understanding of the world. . . ."[6] Hence, in discussing modern Chinese literature, extra-literary criteria as well as the stand of the authors must be taken into account.

The multiple roles of Chinese writers as social critics, political activists, or ideological propagandists will be taken up in greater detail below. Here it is significant to stress that it was precisely their multiple positions that led Chinese writers to impress their literary works with a strong sense of time. This does not mean that one should read modern Chinese literature as it if were a historic or social document, or that this literature does no more than reflect China's social and historic condition at a given time. If this were so, literature would be mere reportage, which may be considered a literary but not an art form. Rather, modern Chinese literature often seems like a record of men and women who relate through fiction their vision of what China is or is not; it is a record of the writers' perception of their reality at a given time, a perception that is rooted in ideological commitment and social and political concern. Problems of individual existence and fate in this literature merge with and cannot be considered apart from the general and the typical. Modern Chinese literature above all illustrates the interaction of the human being and the moment.[7]

Literary works were thus informed by the ideological positions of their authors. When such authors looked to foreign writers and their works and translated these, they did so (among other reasons, of course) with a view toward strengthening their own ideological positions that were taking shape. For this reason, one must necessarily assume that translations were not undertaken at random but that there were principles of selectivity.

It may be useful to clarify here what is meant by intellectuals and writers, and the question of ideology as it relates to literary creativity and translating. This in turn involves understanding the changing position of intellectuals and writers in modern China. Traditionally, intellectuals were part of the official ruling elite. To be sure, some intellectuals throughout Chinese history have withdrawn from the official system either by choice or by force. They could become critics of certain practices or attack what they considered the corrupted values of rulers and society, but in or out of office, their status was that of an educated elite. They were also the writers and the poets. And in spite of the fact that fiction was not considered legitimate literature in traditional China, these literati-intellectuals were the people who produced the great classics of fiction, most often when not in office. In traditional China, therefore, the writer had a different social position than the writer in Western society, who in earliest times was integrated in society and somewhat later moved to dependence on aristocratic patronage.[8] At the end of the nineteenth century, however, the position of Chinese writers and intellectuals changed significantly. Writers became professionals. Two factors were immediately responsible for this change. One was the rejection of tradition, which led numerous intellectuals to renounce the official system of the educated elite. Moreover, the examination system by which an educated man entered the civil service was terminated in 1905. The development of the publishing industry, which allowed writers and intellectuals alike to earn an income from writing, was the second factor that led to the change in Chinese writers' social position. In short, the commercialization of writing led to professionalism. By the 1920s, the professional author, whose livelihood derived from writing, was the accepted mode.

This change to professionalism, however, does not mean that writers abandoned their roles as intellectuals. Writers as intellectuals assumed the role of political and social critics, exponents of change, and often became political activists. Whereas in twentieth-century China not all intellectuals were writers (some, like Liang Ch'i-ch'ao or Hu Shih, may have tried), most writers, as the literate, articulate, and concerned segment of the population, were intellectuals. For this reason, their literary creations reflect their historical concerns, their ideological assumptions, and their preoccupation with the cultural change that they considered themselves to have initiated. Translating, too, was a source of income and was the work of this new group of professionals. And therefore, ideological concerns determined much of what was translated.

In the latter twenties and thirties, writers became increasingly engaged in the political crises of their day. The split between Chiang Kai-shek's Kuomintang and the Communists in particular resulted in differing political commitments among writers and intellectuals. The polarization was exacerbated by the presence of Japan in Manchuria during the first half of the thirties. Chiang Kai-shek's weak response to the foreign danger in Manchuria and North China led to a growing radicalism among intellectuals and writers. Whereas in the latter twenties they saw themselves more and more as part of the vanguard of cultural change, by the thirties many considered themselves as prime movers of the revolution. The interest in oppressed peoples as national and political entities and in the ideas and aspirations expressed in their literary works was due in large measure to the many currents that animated China's intellectuals in the twenties and thirties.

A significantly different picture emerges in the fifties when, after World War II and the civil war in China, translation activity was once more resumed. Literary creativity was now a part of political activity, and a writer's works were subject to political controls. Insistence on ideological conformity demanded that writers and intellectuals relinquish their role as critics. For the past thirty years the government and Communist party have demanded the intellectuals' unqualified support. The position of writers as literary workers has imposed upon them a fundamentally changed outlook, markedly different from that of the twenties and thirties. As a result, oppressed peoples' literature, too, was interpreted in a different light. The notions of oppression, nationalism, or national identity no longer figured in critical discussions about this literature, and those works that were translated were apparently intended to fit into a broad spectrum of translations from world literature.

Translating was at no time considered a random activity, and much has been written in the attempt to define and clarify principles of translation: how one was to translate, why translate, and what to translate. These principles may be summarized as follows. In the fifties and early sixties scholars generally acknowledged that foreign literature in Chinese translation had an impact on the growth of Chinese literature—it provided an opportunity for assimilating the best from other cultures in order to enrich Chinese culture and offered the possibility of contributing to world peace. Frequently, the cultural, rather than the literary, context of translations was stressed. Translating, it was stated, introduces different cultures to one another, and is therefore a cultural function.[9] To justify the need for translating, Liang Ch'i-ch'ao had pointed to historical precedents, the earliest and most extensive of which were the monumental translations of Buddhist writings.[10]

A further question raised was how faithful to the original a Chinese translation need be, considering how different Chinese is from Western languages. In reaction to Lin Shu's (1852-1924) loose translations at the beginning of the twentieth century, it was argued that the trend since the twenties has been to produce faithful translations. The language of these, however, is often so difficult that people cannot understand what they are about. Word for word translation is impossible, and it is useless to insist on not distorting the original text.[11] But if it is altogether impossible to produce word for word translations, then there is the question of what can be omitted and what must be translated. Only after settling this problem can translators decide on the language and style of the Chinese translation.[12]

Concern was also voiced in regard to translators. Can translators produce adequate translations if they are not acquainted with the writings of the experts on Western literature? Will translations not suffer from their limited knowledge of Western literature? Or, in translating, need one not also be aware of the attitude of the original authors?[13] There was, furthermore, the question of audience. To whom were translations addressed? Was there a sufficiently large reading public in the thirties for a journal like I-wen [Translations], for example?[14]

The foregoing brief summary of statements and questions leaves no doubt that Chinese writers and intellectuals were aware that translating into Chinese was a complex undertaking with wider cultural implications.

Oppressed peoples' literature began to be translated only after some aspect of their condition was known to Chinese readers. Interest in the status of oppressed peoples at the end of the nineteenth and the beginning of the twentieth century reflected the endeavor of some Chinese intellectuals to understand imperialist oppression in China and elsewhere. It also reflected their concern with nationalism and national identity. Somewhat different, though related, considerations can be discerned in the large scale translation effort that began around 1918. Interest then in translating from oppressed peoples' literature was not only centered on oppression or maintaining national identity, but also on the renaissance of culture, on creating new culture, on rebirth, and on the importance of authors and their literary works in promoting these views. Translating the literature of oppressed peoples was clearly the product of an era while also being an ingredient in producing an era. In the thirties, renaissance and New Culture paled as the politics of right and left in addition to global conflicts became dominant concerns. These concerns were reflected in discussions on oppressed peoples' conditions, but were only partially reflected in the works chosen for translation. Unlike in the twenties, translations from the literature of oppressed peoples were no longer an ingredient in shaping an era. The large scale translation efforts of the fifties differed substantially from those of previous periods in that oppressed peoples as a topic was no longer a subject of discussion. Moreover, principles of selecting works for translating are not clearly discernible, and it often seems that works were translated as they became available.

The question of numbers of translated works is of considerable importance. Included in this study are short stories, drama, poetry, and some novels. For the most part, I used works that were available to me in Chinese translation as well as in the original, although in some instances I discussed works that I have not seen, but for which I consider the bibliographical listings to be reliable. More translated works may exist than appear in the year by year listing at the end of this study, especially for the fifties (see Appendix A). Unfortunately, both bibliographical resources and actual works are not always available from the People's Republic of China. In assessing the volume of translated items, note must be taken of the repeated publication or retranslation of works. Possibly a number of stories, drama, or poems may have had a wider circulation than would be generally assumed. However, in the twenties, thirties, and fifties, the literate audience was small, and we cannot assume that these translations reached beyond students, their teachers, and a growing urbanized literate public.

From which languages did Chinese translators prepare translations? As a rule, English predominated, although some translators (among these Wang Lu-yen) also used Esperanto. German translations of Central European literature were occasionally resorted to, but it was not until the fifties that German and Russian were more widely used. Irish and black American literature could be translated directly, but Polish and Yiddish literature were obviously retranslations of other translations. Questions of accuracy are not the crucial problem here. Rather, the significant fact is that translating from a translation means that Chinese writers used preselected materials, that is, materials selected by a previous translator. Hence, as far as Polish or Yiddish literature is concerned, choices were more limited than from literatures written in English.

It is further noteworthy that Chinese translators did not choose a representative and wide range of authors. Instead, they tended to select several works by one author, although among these a variety of themes might be chosen. The contrast between the twenties and thirties and the fifties is again significant. Translations from nineteenth-century Polish and Yiddish authors still appeared in the latter period, but at the same time a large number of minor and major twentieth-century Polish writers were being translated, with no attempt being made to present a cross section of their works.

The number of translators was not large. To be sure, quite a few stories were translated under pseudonyms which I was unable to identify, and translators frequently signed only their given names to the translation. Nevertheless, there was a small group of writers who apparently had a sustained interest in translating the literatures of oppressed peoples. I have listed below the major translators, all of whom, it should be noted, were either well-known figures in intellectual life, writers, or literary critics. (For a complete listing of all translators, see Appendix D.)

Chao Ching-shen was a poet, essayist, literary critic, and historian who translated from Irish and black American literature.

Cheng Chen-to was a major figure in the New Literature movement and one of the editors of *Hsiao-shuo yüeh-pao* [Short story monthly]. He is best known for his scholarly work on Chinese literature of all periods and for his many writings on literary theory. His interests in world literature were wide ranging, and he translated a number of essays on literary criticism.

Chou Tso-jen was also a major figure in the New Literature movement and is well known as an essayist. Together with his brother Lu Hsün, he was among the first intellectuals who showed an interest in Eastern European literature, which he translated into Chinese.

Hu Yü-chih was a literary critic and translator who edited several journals, including the *Tung-fang tsa-chih* [Eastern miscellany]. He translated from Polish and Yiddish literature. He actively participated in political life in the People's Republic of China.

Kuo Mo-jo was one of the major figures in modern intellectual history. He was a versatile genius, scholar and historian, poet and writer. In the early twenties, he represented the spirit of romanticism, but soon thereafter he turned to communism. He, like Mao Tun, was an active participant in Chinese cultural life. Kuo's poetry has been widely translated and he is the subject of a book-length study. He translated all of John M. Synge's plays, although there is no evidence that he had a sustained interest in oppressed peoples' literature.

Mao Tun (pseudonym of Shen Yen-ping) wrote and translated under many different names. A prolific author, critic, and translator, Mao Tun is a towering figure in modern Chinese letters. As one of the editors of *Short Story Monthly,* he was instrumental in transforming the journal into one of the most popular and significant organs of modern Chinese literature. Mao Tun was deeply interested in developing theories of modern literary criticism. His interest in Eastern European and oppressed peoples' literature resulted from this concern. His political orientation was increasingly leftist after the mid-twenties, when he joined the Communist party. He continues to be an important figure in Chinese cultural affairs. Mao Tun's short stories and one of his novels have been translated into English, and he is the subject of several scholarly studies.

Wang Lu-yen was the author of many short stories, including children's stories. The majority of his translations were prepared from Esperanto, and he was one of the major translators of Yiddish literature.

Wang T'ung-chao translated under several pseudonyms. Wang belonged to the group of writers who supported *Short Story Monthly*. His translations include works from Irish and Polish literature.

I

THE BACKGROUND: ASPECTS OF CHINA'S LITERARY REVOLUTION AND OPPRESSED PEOPLES, 1900-1920

The closing years of the nineteenth century through May 1919 were eventful years in Chinese history. Following China's defeat in the Sino-Japanese War of 1894-95, intellectual circles engaged in extensive publicist, literary, philosophical, and reformist activities of which the nationalist movement and the 1911 Revolution formed a part. On 4 May 1919, student demonstrations erupted in Peking protesting the decision of the Versailles Peace Conference to cede Shantung province to Japan. The years around 1919 and the twenties were a time of political ferment, of new ideas, of nationalism, and of significant literary productivity. Many ideas propounded after 1895 were redefined and practically applied after 1919. This was true in particular for the so-called Literary Revolution, the roots of which were part of the turn-of-the-century intellectual activity, but which became a major current before and after 1919. The Literary Revolution called for a new Chinese literature, written in the spoken rather than literary language and with a new content.

Chinese translations of Western literary works played a significant role in intellectual and literary life both at the beginning of the twentieth century and twenty-odd years later. Information concerning other countries, their peoples, politics, or histories, was widely disseminated through a flourishing newspaper industry. Also at the end of the nineteenth and beginning of the twentieth century, the first information on the condition of oppressed peoples appeared in the Chinese press. The many translations from their fiction and the critical appraisals published in the twenties resulted from the information that had been made available earlier.

In the following pages, the major developments and ideas relevant to the translating of oppressed peoples' fiction will be

1

traced in chronological order. The more than two decades under
consideration here are enormously rich and complex, but references
of a historical or political nature will be kept to a minimum. The
major aim will be to define the growing interest in oppressed peoples and the intellectual context of which it was a part.

The Treaty Ports and Publishing

That China appeared to enter a new era after 1900 has been
widely noted. Changes were taking place in all aspects of social,
political, and intellectual life.[1] Among these was the spectacular
growth of modern Chinese journalism, especially in the treaty ports.
Publishing was big business, and it was lucrative. Although most
of the newspapers and journals were at first sponsored by Westerners,
control soon gravitated into Chinese hands.[2] The volume of publishing presupposed the existence of a literate or semiliterate reading public in the treaty ports and peripheral areas.

Population also grew rapidly in the treaty ports, particularly
in Shanghai. This growth was the result of an influx into the cities
of industrialists, merchants, and peasant laborers in search of a
better livelihood. In Shanghai, so-called modern schools opened
their doors to Chinese youngsters looking for "new learning."
Teachers, students, revolutionary intellectuals, and reformers
flocked to the treaty ports to become part of the new and stimulating environment.

These students and reformers were greatly influenced by the
new publications. Hu Shih (1891-1962), who has left his imprint on
all areas of modern Chinese intellectual and scholarly life, recalled
years later that when he first went to Shanghai at age fourteen, he
did not let a day pass without reading *Shih-pao* [The Eastern
times], a paper founded in 1904 and which Hu considered to be of
great influence on a generation of students during their formative
years.[3] According to Hu, the greatest merit of *The Eastern Times*
was its brief editorials *(t'uan p'ing)* which were printed in place
of the old-fashioned long essays. Short and to the point, they
were outspoken and presented a variety of views. Readers were
moreover introduced to enjoyable literature and fiction. Hence, a
major feature of the new publications were innovative techniques of
news presentation. The brief editorials referred to by Hu Shih apparently stimulated reader response in the form of letters to the

editor, thereby allowing larger segments of the population to concern themselves with current events.

Possibly the most important innovation, however, was the use
of the vernacular instead of, or in addition to, literary Chinese by
a number of the publications. Among these was the *Wusih pai-hua
pao* [Wusih vernacular], an early pioneering effort which appeared
in 1898. It was followed within a few years by other papers in the
spoken language published in several southern cities. There was
the *Pai-hua pao* [Vernacular journal], a radical paper founded in
1903, whose editors were also engaged in Chekiang revolutionary
activities, and *Ching-yeh hsün-pao* [The struggle], which began
publication in 1906. In addition, several partially vernacular journals addressed to women appeared. Notable examples were the
Nü-hsüeh-pao [Journal of women's studies] and the *Chung-kuo
hsin nü-chieh* [Journal of the new woman of China]. The former
appeared in 1902, first as a supplement to the *Vernacular Journal* and
continued as an independent publication. The latter was established in 1907 and was one of the most successful papers, with a
circulation of seven thousand. These and other papers contained
articles written in both vernacular and literary styles.[4] Although
efforts at reaching large numbers of people by means of the printed
word were more prevalent in the south, the north, too, had a vernacular press, as evidenced by papers such as the *Chihli pai-hua pao*
[Chihli Vernacular]. Papers in the spoken language seemed to have
an educational function as well. For example, a 1905 report mentions a Peking girls' school where the reading of vernacular newspapers was part of the daily curriculum.[5]

The press thus played an important role in bringing about
change in the twentieth century. The language used and the for-
mat in which news was presented was decidedly aimed at attracting
a larger reading public. The content of the news was similarly significant, for, in addition to domestic news, publications of all kinds
regularly featured foreign news. Occasionally, there were notices
of peoples who, like the Chinese, were oppressed by the major
powers. A growing Chinese nationalism demanded a more precise
view of the West, which, in turn, reinforced nationalist and anti-
imperialist sentiments. Gradually, the non-Chinese world came to
be seen as consisting of large and small states, with some of the
latter type deprived of their independence, and of minorities within
states who were without liberties or civil rights. News reporting
regarding these peoples, however, was neither comprehensive nor

up to date. Rather, the foreign news columns and articles are interesting precisely for their selective nature and the kinds of topics they deemed worthy of coverage.

That Poland was a prime example of the dangers of Western imperialism was noted even before the 1890s. Huang Tsun-hsien (1848-1905), statesman and scholar, had referred to Poland's partitioned state in a poem of 1878.[6] Poland's difficulties also received early mention in such publications as the *Hsi-kuo chin-shih hui-pien* [Compendium of recent events in Western countries], especially in 1873, when systematic attempts were made to suppress the Polish language.[7] However, the sorry state of Poland came to be more widely discussed after Liang Ch'i-ch'ao (1873-1929) published his "Account of the Fall of Poland"[8] in 1896 and K'ang Yu-wei (1843-1922) submitted his "Record of the Partition and Fall of Poland"[9] in July 1898 as a memorial to the Kuang-hsü Emperor. The newly founded *Eastern Miscellany* carried a glum article in 1904 on Poland's three partitions (1772, 1793, and 1795) by Russia, Austria, and Prussia, and described the suppression of Polish language and literature and the absence of freedom of speech and publishing. The author compared the fate of China to that of Poland.[10]

The persecution of Jews in Russia, Rumania, and elsewhere was discussed at various times in the *Compendium, Wan-kuo kung-pao* [The globe magazine], and *Min-li pao* [The democrat]. A lengthly article in 1905 tried to explain the activities of the Zionist *(hsün-shan)* organization in connection with the British plan of resettling Jews in East Africa, the so-called Uganda Proposal.[11] Liang Ch'i-ch'ao also voiced concern for the fate of the Jews, and in the account of his travel to the United States in 1903 he recorded his impressions of New York Jews.[12]

Nor did the status of America's black population escape Liang's attention; he believed that in the post-Civil War period blacks were making progress toward greater freedom and rights.[13] Among other publications that described the condition of blacks, *The Globe Magazine* article on Booker T. Washington is noteworthy. Aside from Washington's educational activities generally, his work-study program at Tuskegee and its pedagogic principles were discussed in considerable detail.[14] Not all accounts were complimentary, however. One brief article, for example, stated that even though many of America's blacks are servants and laborers, blacks are naturally disposed toward laziness and indolence. They are incapable of being industrious; they have not contributed leaders, and "some sit in the shade of trees."[15]

Poland's fate under the Russians was frequently compared to British colonialism in India. But Ireland's problem under British domination was seldom mentioned, although *The Democrat* had a number of reports on the 1911 Irish trade union and labor disturbances.[16]

For the first time, the literate Chinese public was exposed to the struggle of other nations and peoples to preserve their national identities, and to the ruthless practices of the major powers in preventing national expression. Chinese readers, furthermore, often found such news in publications that used the more comprehensible vernacular language.

Discussions on Language Reform

The issue of a written vernacular was of central importance to the Literary Revolution; it was also a significant factor in stimulating interest in oppressed peoples' literature. For this reason, it may be useful to briefly recapitulate the various ideas around the turn of the century concerning reform of written Chinese.

The question of how to change or reform the written literary language *(wen-yen* or *ku-wen)*, considered by many to be archaic and cumbersome, was discussed shortly before and after 1900 by various individuals and groups whose motives in advocating reform of written Chinese were quite dissimilar. Christian missionaries wanted to reform the written language in order to promote literacy. A literate church membership would make evangelizing activities more successful. Officials discussed how to simplify written Chinese partly in order to introduce changes in the educational system. A number of intellectuals, among them Liang Ch'i-ch'ao, had more complex motives. A literate public was a prerequisite for transforming China and building a new society. Written and spoken Chinese are like two different languages, they argued, and should be unified. Moreover, in order to advocate programs of reform and change, a new and dynamic terminology must come into use. The issue, however, was not simply to commence using the spoken language in writing, for in fact, vernacular languages were already used in writing. China's language problem was more

complex, involving also the question of how to unify the spoken
vernacular of the south with that of the north.

The missionaries held several views on solving the language
problem. Some missionaries who were active in south China advocated a system of romanization for the various southern dialects,
whereas others maintained that romanizing Chinese could never
obtain wide currency. The majority was in favor of abandoning
characters altogether and of using a phonetic script, with some
suggesting the use of Mandarin *(kuan-hua)*, the written and spoken administrative and business language used throughout northern
China and based on Peking pronunciation, as the standard.[17] Most
stressed the advantage of spoken Chinese and repeatedly emphasized that China needed one common national language.[18]

Aside from the important efforts of Chang Chien (1853-1926),
who headed a national commission to study the problem of a national
(or unified) language *(kuo-yü)*,[19] attempts were made to devise
systems of phonetic transcription. Instead of alphabetizing the
Chinese language, some officials experimented with symbols which
would resemble the Chinese characters themselves. The earliest
such attempt was made by Lu Kan-chang (1854-1928), who tran-
scribed his native Amoy dialect in Latin letters to which he added
phonetic symbols.[20] More important, however, was the Mandarin
Phonetic Alphabet *(Kuan-hua ho-sheng tzu-mu)*, developed by
Wang Chao (1859-1933), which was published in 1900 in Tientsin.
Consisting of parts of Chinese characters, the alphabet had sixty-
two symbols and was based on Peking pronunciation.[21] Eight years
later, Lao Nai-hsüan (1843-1922) enlarged on Wang Chao's efforts
by adapting the latter's symbols to non-Peking dialects. After the
establishment of the Republic in 1912, these and other phonetic
systems were combined into a Standard Phonetic Alphabet *(Kuo-
yin tzu-mu)*.

The issue of how to relate language to literature, however,
was not raised in any of these discussions and proposals. Also
neglected was the fact that the vernacular in various parts of China
had been used for some time in the writing of fiction.[22] Liang
Ch'i-ch'ao's call to write in the common language *(li-yü)*, therefore,
was the exception rather than the rule.[23] That language reform,
whatever its nature, could not be considered in isolation, but
had to be seen as related to the writing of literature, was widely
stated only some years later. Moreover, in the early years of
the twentieth century, calls for language reform from various

quarters were not coordinated with, for example, the actual use of vernacular in the press. In spite of the awareness that China's written language had to be modified to accomodate change, a self-conscious statement on the inseparability of language and literature was not made until the Literary Revolution of the teens. Such a statement, in turn, demanded agreement on a commonly accepted written vernacular, which occurred only much later.

Aspects of the Literary Scene in the Early 1900s

A number of factors were responsible for the enormous increase of fictional works after 1900. Among these, the growing publishing industry is again of major importance. Many of the new journals and newspapers began to add literary supplements *(fu-k'an)*, which in time became full-fledged literary journals. It was in these that much of contemporary fiction was published in serialized form. According to Hu Shih, the new literary works (though not of very high quality) were avidly read by the younger generation.[24]

Another major factor was the significance that Liang Ch'i-ch'ao and others began attributing to the function of fiction in the new era. Fiction, traditionally considered as inferior to other literary forms, was no longer to be a literary stepchild; it was to become a respectable art form and a tool for changing China. In a widely read essay which appeared in 1902, Liang wrote:

> If one wishes to renew the people of a country,
> one cannot but first renew its fiction. There-
> fore, wishing to renew morality, it is necessary
> to renew fiction. Wishing to renew government
> . . . customs . . . [or] study of the arts, it is
> necessary to renew fiction.[25]

Other writers enthusiastically seconded Liang's call for giving fiction its proper place, some arguing for a reexamination of traditional fiction and others for understanding more clearly the social context of fiction. Liang ascribed special importance to the genre of political fiction, a genre he considered of prime importance in the transformation of Europe. Furthermore, he had observed at first hand the important role literary works had in influencing the implementation of reforms in Japan.[26]

Although Liang himself had a fair number of dubious fictional works to his credit, it was the authors of satirical social criticism, adventure, and emotion, written for the greater part in vernacular, that captured the popular imagination. The impressive production of such fiction, which had obvious entertainment value, was most likely due to its marketability and the profits publishers realized from it. But Liang Ch'i-ch'ao and other intellectuals encouraged a more serious interest in fiction, for fiction, they felt, should be considered as legitimate a literary form as, say, poetry. Hence, by publishing literary journals and including serialized novels in their publications, they hoped to remove the stigma traditionally attached to fiction.

The large quantity of translations from Western fiction at this time must be seen as an integral part of literary production. No doubt increased contacts with Westerners in the treaty ports played a major role in stimulating interest in translating Western fiction, although the profit motive in publishing translations was also important. Publishers would not have printed translations had they not sold. In his study on Lin Shu, Compton points out that translators selected materials for translating in accordance with what was familiar. They looked for an interesting story. Generally, authors and themes were selected that complemented the vernacular novels of adventure or emotion that were manufactured in the treaty ports. The purpose of translating was not to introduce new elements into Chinese literature, Compton found, and Western fiction was not appreciated for its literary value.[27]

Translations, often more a loose paraphrase, from the works of such authors as Charles Dickens, Conan Doyle, H. Rider Haggard, Victor Hugo, and Robert Louis Stevenson predominated. Some carried moral messages, but for the most part they were read for entertainment. Without exception, these were works from major literatures. Whatever image Chinese readers might have obtained of the West via these translations, it was probably not as important as the knowledge that the West, too, had a literary tradition. The translations appeared both in vernacular and literary Chinese. Lin Shu used the literary style exclusively, whereas Su Man-shu (1884–1918) —a truly colorful personality of the period who introduced Byron to Chinese readers—frequently used southern vernacular for his translations. Apparently Chinese readers showed no preference for translations in either the vernacular or literary style; both types were read. Also, translations were prepared selectively and

serious works of nineteenth-century Western realism were not translated at this time. The discovery of the realistic and romantic traditions in Western fiction took place some years later and was at
that time joined with the nationalistic and revolutionary concerns
that animated the seething Chinese student community in Japan.

Early Notices of the Literature of Oppressed Peoples

Chinese nationalism prior to 1912 consisted of a variety of
elements. Anti-imperialism, reassertion of Chinese power, modernization, China for the Chinese—all these were nationalist issues propounded as radical or conservative tenets. Although the treaty
port setting provided manifold possibilities for expressing nationalist sentiments, it was in Japan that the more radically inclined
found refuge from the Ch'ing government's repressive measures.
Many also went to Japan in search of new learning, since new or
Western knowledge via the Japanese medium was considered necessary for solving China's problems. Emotions often ran high. Na-
tionalists and revolutionaries, conservatives and radicals were not
a sober, cool-headed lot. That Western literature and Western
writers did receive attention in Japan may be in part, at least, attributed to the charged atmosphere of the Chinese student community. The well-known essayist Chou Tso-jen (1885-1966), who
arrived in Japan in 1906, recollected years later:

> Originally I studied sea transportation, and I had
> few opportunities to relate this to literature.
> Later, because of my enthusiasm for the problem
> of national revolution, I went to hear Chang
> T'ai-yen's lectures.[28] At that time Mr. Chang
> regularly incited against the Manchus, and he
> lectured on this topic. Later on again, because
> I paid attention to the literature of national revo-
> lution, I connected this literature with that of
> weak and small peoples. Among all kinds of
> works, like those of the Dutch, the Poles, the
> Jews and the Indians, there were some which
> described the country's internal decadent con-
> ditions. There were some which described the
> deeply grievous loss of their country's indepen-
> dence. And when I read these, they had a deep

effect on me, because they also made highly
interesting reading.[29]

Two points in Chou's statement need to be stressed. One was the
sympathetic response to national revolution and national oppression
in other countries and, secondly, the appeal of this theme in a
literary medium.

Chou Tso-jen's brother, Lu Hsün (Chou Shu-jen, 1881-1936),
who had come to Japan in 1902, also read this literature. When he
discovered the Polish poet Adam Mickiewicz (1798-1855), he concluded that Poland's political impotence in the nineteenth century
led to a time of unsurpassed literary creativity. In spite of greatest
darkness, the human spirit reasserted itself through literature,
heralding a new era. In Mickiewicz Lu Hsün saw a poet-patriot
and activist, an unconventional man who attempted to arouse his
people to new life. There were others, such as the Hungarian
Sandor Petöfi (1822-1849), Byron and Shelley in England, and
Lermentov and Pushkin in Russia. Lu Hsün designated them Mara
poets. They teach China, wrote Lu Hsün in 1907, that the coming
of the new tide (hsin-ch'ao) cannot be halted; a new culture (hsin
wen-hua) will come to China. [30] The appearance of great men brings
about a cultural awakening, wrote Lu Hsün. Years later, he recalled
that the nationalist literature of countries like Poland had attracted
his attention because in spite of being small countries, they had an
exceptionally large number of writers. [31]

Arguing that literature and art had a role in social transformation, the Chou brothers undertook to translate a collection of
Western short stories into Chinese.[32] The book appeared in Japan
in 1909 under the title of *Yü-wai hsiao-shuo chi* [Collection of foreign short stories]. Among the twenty-eight stories, only ten pro-
perly belong to the literature of oppressed peoples; the majority
were translated from Russian, German, Scandinavian, and other
literatures.[33] The book, which appeared in literary Chinese, was
not a success and sold barely a few copies. Its failure, however,
need not be ascribed to the literary language, since both translated and original fiction was published in literary as well as in
vernacular Chinese. Rather, it may be assumed that the message
of nationalism and revolution in these stories together with the
technique of realism was as yet too novel to be popularly accepted.
The *Collection* was a pioneering effort which bore fruit only ten-odd
years later during the May Fourth period and the Literary Revolution.

Discussions on Language and Literature among
Chinese Students in America

When America returned the Boxer Indemnity to China in 1908,
stipulating that a scholarship fund be established with the money,
Chinese students began to flock to American colleges and universi-
ties. As a group, this student generation had been influenced in
adolescence by Liang Ch'i-ch'ao's stormy calls for change and renewal. As youngsters they were also exposed to innovative styles
of news reporting, as mentioned by Hu Shih, and to various types
of fiction as well as translations from Western literature. Many
came from the treaty ports where they had attended schools that
offered "new learning" together with traditional studies. By and
large, the generation of Chinese students that went to study in the
United States had absorbed new ideas and new ways of thinking
from their teachers and their environment. As they embarked on
their studies in America, their expectations regarding their future
role in changing China were no doubt already different from those
of Liang's generation. The importance of this generational difference must be stressed.

Equally significant is the fact that when Chinese students
arrived on the American college campus, they at once came into contact with American student activism and the ferment of a spectrum
of divergent ideas. The "American mode," it has been argued,
emerged when John Dewey, George Santayana, and William James
began to be heard intellectually, and when mass-circulated maga-
zines began to publicize culturally new literary trends and contrary
political opinions.[34] Many Chinese students were caught up in the
excitement of campus life. This atmosphere, together with their
earlier experiences in various, often revolutionary societies, quite
likely contributed toward the development of an active Chinese student life. They established Chinese student clubs, held regional
summer conferences and supported publications like *The Chinese
Student's Monthly*. Free discussion and open controversy were
regular features of their campus life. The American campus was
preeminently conducive to discussing China's problems.

Among the topics of debate was the question of language.
Aside from some tentative proposals for alphabetization, occasioned
by the suggestion that Chinese emulate the Korean alphabet system,[35] Chinese students discussed at length the problems of teach-
ing Chinese and especially the writing of literature. By raising

the issue of literary creativity in conjunction with promoting literacy, alphabetizing Chinese became increasingly less attractive.

Between the summer of 1915 and spring 1916, a group of Chinese students, among whom Hu Shih assumed a kind of leadership, discussed the question of language and literature with mounting intensity. The theoretical assumptions of the Literary Revolution gradually took shape when language and literature were seen to function within a historical context and when the notion of historical progress in literature (li-shih-ti wen-hsüeh chin-pu) was held to be of basic significance.[36] Hu's argument is worth recapitulating. The form of the written language, he stated, is the instrument of literature. Once the instrument becomes nonfunctional (whether as prose or poetry), meanings are no longer clearly expressed. Throughout history, literary changes have resulted from new uses of language because "the life of literature is completely dependent on the use of a contemporary live instrument which represents the emotions and thoughts of that time." In Chinese history, language and literature had changed several times. These changes may be called literary revolutions, of which the use of the vernacular (li-yü) since the Yüan dynasty (1280-1368) has been the most significant.[37] According to Hu, the live vernacular language today is pai-hua (the northern vernacular) and the dead nonfunctional language still used at the present time for literary purposes is ku-wen. Therefore, the task for the present is to substitute pai-hua for ku-wen. By August 1916, Hu Shih had developed his eight-point program for literary reform, which he mailed to Ch'en Tu-hsiu (1879-1942) in Peking in the middle of October. His "Tentative Proposals for the Reform of Literature" ("Wen-hsüeh kai-liang ch'u-i") was published in Hsin ching-nien [New youth] in January 1917.

Although the above summary has dealt solely with Hu Shih's views, it should be remembered that he developed his ideas in debate and controversy with others to whom he gave full credit in his writings. The debates on several points reflect clearly the American intellectual scene. Among others, the ideas of the Columbia historian James Harvey Robinson are possibly the most prominent and influential.[38] In his lectures as well as his works, Robinson championed two specific ideas which Hu Shih applied to China. One was that the present cannot be understood without searching out its roots in the past. The other was that the present age represents the emergence of the true democratic spirit as expressed in respect and appreciation for the common human being.[39] The first led Hu to an examination of the history of Chinese literature in order to understand the present concern with change. The second reaffirmed for him the need for mass literacy and the termination of elitist literature.

Thus, by 1917, language and literature were inseparably joined and the vernacular was defined as *pai-hua* and as having had a historical development. With the beginning of the May Fourth movement in China, these and other ingredients were combined in the Literary Revolution. The issue of language and literature was, of course, also an important consideration in regard to oppressed peoples' literature. After translations began to appear, it was pointed out time and again that the new use of language by oppressed peoples led to an upsurge of literary creativity and to a change in their condition.

May Fourth and the Literary Revolution

The student demonstrations against China's humiliation by Japan at the Versailles Peace Conference began on 4 May 1919, sparking a nationwide protest movement. As it gradually involved political, intellectual, economic, social, and cultural issues, May Fourth became a turning point in modern Chinese history. The Literary Revolution, the goals and assumptions of which had been defined more precisely in the past two decades in China as well as among Chinese abroad, became a part of this broad stream of reform.

Several achievements are significant for the Literary Revolution during the May Fourth period. The vernacular *(pai-hua)* was adopted as the written language by new publications as well as by the older newspapers and journals. Spreading rapidly among all segments of Chinese society, by 1921 the vernacular was recognized officially as China's written language. A new literature with new content and using innovative techniques began to appear, and new writers began to question and examine old and new literary theories. Both the use of vernacular and the writing of literature were seen as cultural and political activities aimed at changing Chinese society. At the same time, a large number of new journals with a broad cultural, political, and literary orientation began to appear, and it was in these that translations of oppressed peoples' literature were featured.

That literature was politically significant had been noted earlier by Liang Ch'i-ch'ao when he called attention to the genre of political fiction. Ch'en Tu-hsiu reiterated this point while emphasizing the relationship between literature and society in a brief and wildly enthusiastic article of February 1916. In it, Ch'en called for the creation of a "literary revolution army" which would have three aims: to produce people's instead of gentry literature, realistic literature instead of classics, and popular instead of "recluse" literature.[40] However, Ch'en's interest in the vernacular movement, as Richard Kagan has argued, concerned political processes and how to change society. Thus the social class that had created the old literature had also infused its language with decadent notions.[41] To Ch'en, literature operated within the broad context of Chinese culture and society, an idea he restated more forcefully than Liang had done. And together with the *New Youth* group, Ch'en identified political change with cultural change. Unless culture itself (that is, morality, social values, literature, art, language) changed, political change would remain ineffective. Prior to 1921 and before he turned increasingly to Marxist theory, Ch'en asserted the limitations of political revolution. These considerations, however, lead to aspects of the New Culture movement, which will be discussed in a different context in the following chapter.

Literary Revolutionists asserted the political nature and function of literature in regard to both new and traditional literature. Numerous older works, especially China's great novels, were scrutinized not only for their lively style and vernacular usage, but also for their social and political importance. On the other hand, early twentieth-century writings which had appeared in large quantities in the treaty ports were often harshly criticized.[42] New literature, they argued, was not merely to entertain or tell a good story, as did the literature of the past two decades.

In addition to its social and political function, the new literature was to contribute toward standardizing and unifying the spoken language. The problem of regional spoken Chinese had not been solved by adopting *pai-hua* for writing Chinese. It was hoped that a standard national language *(kuo-yü)* would evolve with the writing of *kuo-yü* literature. According to Hu Shih, the development of a national language is inseparable from literary creativity; "it is impossible to standardize a language the use of which is barred from the literary works of the age," and literature, "not any pronouncing alphabet or pronouncing dictionaries . . . will eventually standardize the spoken language,"[43] he declared in 1919. Hu also raised the slogan "A literature in the national language, and a literary national language" *(kuo-yü-ti wen-hsüeh, wen-hsüeh-ti kuo-yü)*.

Chou Tso-jen saw the basis of the new literature in its human orientation, and, like Ch'en Tu-hsiu, he pointed to the importance of realism. New literature is significant, he wrote, because it is human literature *(jen-ti wen-hsüeh)*, which is realistic; and while highlighting the particular, the new literature should have universal human implications as well.[44]

Chou's statements reflect the closeness of intellectual and literary issues. His interest in Western literary realism first developed in Japan and continued after his return to China. After 1917, Chou's views were shared by increasingly larger circles of intellectuals and writers. Furthermore, when Chou attempted to define the universal and the particular in literary creation, he indicated his and others' growing desire to see new Chinese literature in a worldwide context. If Chinese writers, in creating new literature, accepted the centrality of human beings—the lives, joys, sorrows, or aspirations of common people—they would be writing in a particular way about particular Chinese, as others were doing elsewhere. Therefore, by wanting Chinese literature to be in and a part of the world, Chou necessarily went on to stress the importance of translating from world literature. Universality was knowing and understanding the particularity of others.

Reflections on universalism and particularism were a part of New Culture thinking and had a part in the Literary Revolution. Hence, universality and particularity must also be seen in conjunction with the introduction of Western literary theories into China. This topic has been ably discussed by several authors and only some relevant points need to be mentioned here.

Modern Chinese literary criticism began with the inquiry into nineteenth-century Western literary theories. Therefore, at the inception of twentieth-century Chinese literary criticism were investigations of issues distant in place as well as in time. Because literature was conceived as functioning within culture, issues of literary criticism involved not only the formulation of new criteria for evaluating literature, but also new attitudes to reality and new ways of perceiving the world. Literary criticism, therefore, forged a close connection between literary and intellectual value with aesthetic value becoming a secondary consideration.[45] Chinese writers attempted to incorporate into their approaches to Chinese literature the theories of romanticism, neo-romanticism, realism, and naturalism. But considerable confusion existed even among Western critics as to the precise definition of each.

> The concept of romanticism was associated with the cause of national liberation, individualism and democracy, as well as with subjectivism, primitivism and irrationality. Realism was variously seen as a descriptive technique, a literary movement and a philosophical outlook, while naturalism was sometimes equated with realism and sometimes described as a narrow or "scientific" version of it. Neo-romanticism was most commonly seen as a compound of realism and romanticism . . . [and] it also appeared under the labels of neo-idealism and neo-heroism.[46]

This confusion of movements and concepts was transmitted to Chinese intellectuals and writers and accounts for the frequent contradictions found in their writings.

Aside from Chou Tso-jen, whose views have been mentioned, Mao Tun, one of modern China's foremost writers, also wrote extensively on literary theory. Where Hu Shih spoke of the evolution of the Chinese language and literature, Mao Tun stressed the universal evolutionary process in all literatures, although its occurrence varies with time and place. Like Chou Tso-jen, Mao Tun asserted the importance of the life of humankind in literature, but he gave special weight to "social background" and the spirit of the age in literature. Mao Tun's views on realism (or naturalism—he did not always distinguish between the two) is significant, for he saw realism not as an end but as a transitional stage or in combination with romanticism. Recognizing the shortcomings of realism as a literary technique, his focus in the early twenties was on the perception of reality by the writer and its artistic transformation or reflection in literature.[47]

The concept of "art for art's sake," although briefly advocated, did not have an impact either at this or a later time; that literature serves a variety of purposes was taken for granted. Most Literary Revolutionists, moreover, stressed the wider, universal implications of their endeavor while addressing themselves to particular problems in Chinese literature. With boundless optimism Chinese writers appropriated the world instead of retreating from it. This is possibly one of the most impressive features of this period.

Translating and the Literary Revolution

Since practically all of the major writers and intellectuals stressed the importance of translating works from world literature, they also initiated the task of translating. Unlike twenty-odd years earlier, which had also been a time of intensive translating activity, translations now were undertaken as a purposeful program and the reasons for doing so were repeatedly explained.

Translating from world literature was to Chou Tso-jen the reaffirmation of particularism within universalism. All cultures express themselves through literature, but each culture's literature is particularly expressed. The importance of "human literature" lies in its concern with universal experiences of men and women. By translating foreign literature, Chinese will understand the lives of humankind, according to Chou. Some years later, in his introduction to *Hsüeh-jen* [The snowman], Mao Tun echoed Chou Tso-jen when he stated that although the stories he had translated in this volume are varied in nature and dissimilar in content, they have one element in common, namely, their humanistic inquiry.[48]

These new writers and intellectuals also believed that translating foreign literature will stimulate the creation of valid Chinese literature. The May 1921 "Wen-hsüeh hsün-k'an hsüan-yen" [Manifesto of the Literary Ten daily] stated that bringing world literature to China will give Chinese literature new life and will begin efforts to create a new Chinese literature.[49] According to Mao Tun, the objectives of the new literature movement cannot be realized without understanding the literary movements of other peoples. Such understanding, he felt, will lead to the actual creation of new literature.[50] Hu Shih in 1922 similarly attached great importance to the translating of foreign literature. In his view, it was the second aspect of the new phase in the Literary Revolution; the first aspect had been initiated with the writing of vernacular poetry.51

Like at the turn of the century, when publishing in the treaty ports was directly related to the upsurge of literary and translation activity, the proliferation of largely vernacular journals in the May Fourth movement also played a major role in advancing the Literary Revolution. There were differences, however. Although publishing was still concentrated in Shanghai, many of the new publications appeared elsewhere, notably in Peking and Tientsin. Whereas earlier the commercial aspect of publishing—that is, the profit motive— was a factor, many of the new publications in the May Fourth period were student and intellectual ventures, launched by activists at the University of Peking and at Tientsin's Tsinghua University. As such, their publication schedule was often irregular and many were short-lived. Furthermore, turn-of-the-century publications were in the main newspapers and tabloids, although a number regularly featured special supplements. In contrast, the May Fourth publications consisted largely of journals with a broad cultural-political orientation; newspaper supplements also proliferated. Many journals were sponsored by literary societies, formed for the purpose of supporting specific literary trends. Most of the journals, literary or otherwise, featured translations on a fairly regular basis, the translations chosen for inclusion often reflecting the personal proclivities of the editors. Finally, the various new publications now addressed themselves to a broader spectrum of Chinese society: intellectuals, students, provincial teachers, merchants, the literate middle class, workers, as well as radicals from all walks of life were included in the readership.

As part of the Literary Revolution, and whose editors and contributors fashioned the content and course of the new literature, some of these publications deserve brief mention. *Short Story Monthly* was edited by the Literary Association *(Wen-hsüeh yen-chiu hui)*, which was formed in 1920 by a group of Peking writers. From 1921 on, the journal was extremely influential in championing realistic literature and in publishing works by young and unknown writers. According to the editorial policy of the journal, it featured translations, world literary news, and biographical sketches of foreign writers in addition to new works by Chinese writers. Publication ceased in 1932 when the premises of Commercial Press were bombed out.

New Youth, founded in 1915, published translations from its very inception. Until 1918, these were in the literary as well as vernacular style and thereafter changed completely to the vernacular. The journal was an influential organ of the May Fourth movement and the Literary Revolution. When its contents and editorial policy became increasingly political after 1922, the literary content and translations decreased.

Eastern Miscellany, which began publication in 1904, underwent reorganization in 1920, part of which was to include literary materials and translation. As one of the oldest journals, and with its liberal editorial policy under Hu Yü-chih, it had a wide circulation. A fairly large number of articles concerned with Western literary theory appeared in its pages.

Among important literary supplements, there were the *Ch'en pao fu-k'an* [Morning post supplement] and *Wen-hsüeh chou pao* [Literary weekly]. The *Morning Post* had been established by Liang Ch'i-ch'ao and others. Between 1919 and 1923, when the supplement was edited by Sun Fu-yüan, a large number of translations were included. *The Literary Weekly*, which began publication in 1921 in Shanghai as a supplement to the *Shih-shih hsin pao* [China times], appeared under this title beginning in 1923 in Peking. Through the mid-twenties it remained one of the most significant publications next to *Short Story Monthly*. The bulk of the translations and critical articles appeared in these journals and supplements. Their editors and contributors were also the translators and critics, and, of course, they were the leading intellectuals of the various movements of the May Fourth period. Of these, the New Culture movement is most relevant to the topic of this study.

II

NEW CULTURE, RENAISSANCE, AND IMAGES OF OPPRESSED PEOPLES IN THE TWENTIES

The 1920s in China was an era of intense efforts at political, social, intellectual, and literary change. Students and their teachers were at the center of the ferment. Various movements and associations proliferated; there were political study groups and literary societies. Among these, the so-called New Culture movement held a prominent place. Not really a movement in the conventional sense—Joseph T. Chen has suggested the term "thought movement" (in distinction to "action")[1]—its avowed goal was no less than the transformation of the entire fabric of Chinese culture: social and personal mores, values, art, literature, language or scholarship, and even political forms. New Culturists did not consider themselves to be breaking with China's past, but rather as moving the old culture into a new and dynamic present.

Frequently they defined their proposals for a new culture in terms of a Chinese renaissance. The term "renaissance" was of course borrowed from the West where it is used to designate the historical period between the fourteenth and sixteenth centuries, marked especially by the revival of classical influence. As used by the New Culturists, however, the term renaissance assumed a variety of meanings which often had little, if any, relationship to the content of the European Renaissance.[2]

Some writers also referred to a renaissance among oppressed peoples. They, like the Chinese in the twentieth century, were considered by Chinese writers to have had a renaissance in the nineteenth century while searching for new culture. An enormous amount of literary creativity resulted from this search and was an aspect of their renaissance. There were two views, then, concerning the Chinese renaissance: one comparing events in China around 1920 to the European Renaissance of several centuries earlier, and

the other identifying Chinese efforts with nineteenth-century nationalist and literary activity. Both of these views will be explored
in some detail.

The Renaissance: Two Views

China's twentieth-century renaissance, it was argued, most
clearly resembled the European Renaissance, which was the revival
of literature and art *(wen-i fu-hsing)* in the West. According to
Hu Shih, the journalist Huang Yüan-yung has, as early as 1915,
compared China's needs to those of Europe at the time of the
Renaissance when the average man entered the scene and medieva-
lism was overthrown.[3] Therefore, Huang concluded, China's awakening is dependent on the initiation of a renaissance. At about the
same time, Hu himself pointed out that the scientific inventions of
Newton and Edison and the ideas of Bacon and Shakespeare had
qualities of renewal and therefore led to the new tide *(hsin-ch'ao)*
in Europe.[4] To Chiang Mon-lin (1886-1964), in turn, the significance of the European Renaissance consisted primarily of the development of a new attitude to life and human nature and the beginning
of new cosmological ideas. The social and political effects of these
new concepts culminated in twentieth-century democracy.[5]

Many writers tended to emphasize the relevance of the notion
of renaissance to Chinese literature. Hu Shih had done so in 1917.
The real importance of the European Renaissance, he wrote, was
the beginning of the use of vernacular literature in every country.
Latin was abandoned, and writers like Dante and Petrarch adopted
the spoken language *(kuo-yü)*.[6] A number of years later Wang
Che-fu stated:

> A comparison of the new literature movement
> and the European Renaissance is not inappro-
> priate . . . because, although they are long
> separated in time and space, from the stand-
> point of literary history, they are both a
> glorious page. . . . Therefore, there are peo-
> ple who take China's new literature movement
> and designate it as a renaissance. . . .

Wang went on to say that there is only one difference between the
European Renaissance and the Chinese new literature movement;

the first was a case of returning to Greek learning while the second, through the *ku-wen* school, pioneered vernacular *(kuo-yü)* literature.[7] When Wang thus compared the European Renaissance to the new literature movement, he echoed the views of New Culturists who had come to regard the new literature of the Literary Revolution as the cornerstone of New Culture. Here again, it was Hu Shih who stated this view most forcefully. The leaders of the New Culture movement, he declared in a lecture, "want a new language, a new literature, a new outlook on life and society, and a new scholarship."[8] In sum, New Culture, like the European Renaissance, would be China's road to modernity.

> The Renaissance is, of course, the term usually associated with that great movement in Western history which heralded modern Europe. The same name has been accorded to the far reaching changes in thought and action which have swept over China during the last ten years. . . .[9]

Not all writers compared the literary and intellectual ferment in China of the twenties to the Renaissance of several hundred years earlier. Instead, they compared the China of their day to the nineteenth-century national awakening among oppressed peoples in Europe. And they underscored the relationship between the political fact of national assertion and literary productivity in both nineteenth-century Europe and twentieth-century China.

Chinese writers have stated that Slavic literature underwent a renaissance *(fu-huo)* in the second half of the nineteenth century, bringing with it the first stirrings of national assertion. Not only Slavic peoples, but Irish, Jews, and Hungarians also awakened to a renaissance *(fu-hsing)* and experienced an increase in literary productivity; the Czechs, emphasized Lu Hsün, were especially noteworthy in this respect.[10] As a result of their renaissance, these peoples gained new hope which China must also acquire. Cheng Chen-to explained that the Irish literary renaissance was similarly important because the demand for political independence and freedom was made in conjunction with literary and artistic accomplishments.[11]

According to these views, the primary aspects of a renaissance were political and national, although neither precluded cultural change. Setting up the renaissance of nineteenth-century

Europe as a model had the distinct advantage of it being closer in time to the China of the New Culture movement. The people and issues of oppressed peoples' renaissances had substance and immediacy.

The two views outlined above were, however, not contradictory. Western examples were resorted to in both cases, and the notion of a turning point which would usher in sweeping changes were common to both. The significance of the latter view should be sought in its implied political message, which, by focusing on particular renaissances, also pointed to the importance of particular national literatures. Franz Kafka in a diary notation of December 1911 referred to such literatures as "the keeping of a diary by a nation"; a small nation's literature represents "the spiritualization of the broad area of public life." And perhaps Chou Yang (b. 1908), the man most responsible for contemporary China's literary policy, had a similar thought when he mentioned how fortunate it was that the works of small and weak peoples influenced Chinese literature in the May Fourth period.[12]

Bearing in mind that the topic of Poles, blacks, or Jews was not entirely new in journalistic accounts (reports of their condition having appeared earlier) the next four sections will examine in greater detail the way the renaissances were perceived.

Polish Nationalism and Polish Literature

The view that there is an inherent connection between Poland's struggle for national independence and literary productivity was derived from works in English, German, or French which dealt either wholly or in part with Polish literature. Articles in Chinese were either summaries of such works or translations of chapters considered to be significant.

Thus, a chapter from Emile Faguet's *Initiation Littéraire* (1913) provided information on nationalism, language, and literature. According to Faguet (in Chinese translation), Poland, in spite of losing her independence in the eighteenth century, experienced a literary renaissance *(wen-hsüeh fu-hsing)* in the nineteenth century. The people preserved the Polish language, thereby allowing later writers to launch a national literature.[13] Jan de Holewinski's *An Outline of the History of Polish Literature* (1916) furnished information on the extent to which Poland's literary figures contributed to the struggle for national independence. Chou Tso-jen's reading of Holewinski led him to conclude that ideological and literary movements have a counterpart in politics. According to Holewinski's explanation, ideological romanticism declined in Poland after the 1863 insurrection, when the flower of Polish manhood was imprisoned or exiled. Then, August Comte's positivism, an import from abroad, led to a new spirit in Polish letters, as exemplified in Eliza Orzeszkowa's novels. Positivism lost its force, however, when writers like Maria Konopnicka and Henryk Sienkiewicz began to write a true literature of the people. No doubt much influenced by the intensive Russian and Prussian cultural suppression of Poland during the 1880s, writers like Sienkiewicz turned increasingly to the rediscovery of the national past. Thus, the plight of the peasantry and the riches of the national heritage became the central motifs in these writers' works.[14]

The Chinese translation of a Japanese essay on Polish literature stressed the emotional quality of Polish literature. Polish authors, it was stated, are always moved by Poland's national destiny; in their works they do not forget that there is a Polish nation. This unique Polish spirit—a spiritual vitality (ching-shen) and national consciousness—is manifested in the country's scholarship, art, and literature.[15]

In considering nationalism and national self-expression a major motivating force in the emergence and development of modern Polish literature, Chinese writers tended to look askance at the efforts of younger and contemporary Polish writers. Shen Yü was frankly appalled at these writers' unbridled individualism and their demand for freedom of literary creativity. The rejection of nationalism in the so-called modernists' works and their emphasis on universalism and world culture, he wrote, has caused Polish literature to lag in the twentieth century.[16]

Shen Yü's criticism is easily understandable. Most Chinese writers on Poland, its literature and culture, felt that nationalism needed to remain a force in the country's life even after independence. Chang Wei-tz'u, who frequently commented on Polish affairs, wrote admiringly of Poland's rebirth (fu-huo) and of the strength of the Polish culture which had been crucial in the people's rejection of foreign cultural influences. However, the country faces complex problems of social and national integration, he wrote in 1922, and the Poles seem incapable of keeping their goal in focus.[17]

In their choices of chapters to translate and in their essays, Chinese writers showed a unique sensitivity to the role Polish writers had played in giving substance and support to Polish nationalism. According to one commentator, "The nation, deprived of its political institutions, had no other channels of free expression but art and writing. And it was not unnatural that writers and artists became generally regarded as leaders of the national spirit."[18] The importance of art, especially music, in Poland's national renaissance was noted by several Chinese writers when they referred to Chopin's role as a composer and Paderewski's as a musician.[19] Moreover, the importance of the Polish language as the means for creating a national literature was not overlooked in China. For indeed, as Coleman points out, Polish as a literary language only gained ground after the partition of the country in the late eighteenth century, when writers began to utilize Polish in order to instill into their people a sense of nationhood.[20] Hence, in Poland, like in China, transforming a largely spoken language into a literary tool was considered of major importance to national awakening. Finally, when Chinese writers ascribed great significance to the late nineteenth-century Polish literary movement as a whole, they were certainly not off the mark. For, in addition to its political and nationalist function, this movement represented a literary revolution as well as an important current in Polish intellectual life.[21]

Zionism as a Renaissance Movement

According to Chinese writers, a renaissance of the Jewish nation occurred when Jews developed a new culture and a new language and literature. Information on Jews was obtained from Japanese, German, American, or British sources. Newspapers, including Jewish papers like the New York *Jewish Tribune*, were one source, books another. But apparently only a small number of books on Jewish history and Jews was available and most of the sources used were not written by Jews.[22]

Practically all of the articles stressed the fact of the Jews' dispersion and emphasized that the Zionist movement was an organized effort to help their return to the homeland *(ku-hsiang* or *chia-hsiang)*. World War I was considered a turning point in their

condition.[23] At times, unsuspecting Chinese authors were misled
by their materials, especially when these utilized anti-Semitic writings. A straightforward statement on the Zionist movement might,
therefore, also include such a contrary notion as Freemasonry
being a principle of Zionism, which wants "to uphold the Zionist
system of monarchy, and to construct the whole world as a great
Jewish kingdom."[24] Occasionally Chinese authors pointed out that
Jewish activities in the various countries were mainly concerned
with commerce and trade, and therefore, the Zionist aim of making
agricultural workers out of Jews would be an immense task of re-
education. In this connection, the Soviet attempt to retrain Jews
for agriculture was also discussed.[25] In addition to Jewish pre-
dominance in trade, many Jews were highly educated, capable and
intelligent, and there was no illiteracy. Much of this information
was supplied as background, together with some historical data,
such as the geographic location of Palestine, the Jewish monarchy
in history, the Jews' problems with the Greeks and Romans, and
their exile from their land of origin. Some information on Jewish
religion was also included in the accounts. The fact that Jews have
not abandoned religious practices, which has led to their being one
of the oppressed and persecuted peoples in the world,was mentioned
as well.

The Zionist party (Chi-an hui) was usually described as a
renaissance movement (fu-hsing yün-tung).[26] It was organized in
response to persecution suffered and in order to protect the Jewish
cultural heritage. The purpose of the party was to help Jews in
all matters and to assist their return to Palestine so they could
begin new lives. Returning to Palestine served both political and
cultural purposes: the political goal was to construct a Jewish
national state,[27] and the cultural goal was to develop the special
characteristics of the Jewish people. For this reason, they
resisted assimilation with Arabs, particularly since Jews considered
their culture to be of a higher order. For this reason, too, Jews
want to perpetuate their own teachings and their own education
in Palestine.[28]

The Zionist party as a movement produced a Jewish renaissance in Palestine. The Jews were helped by the British with the
Balfour Declaration of November 1917.[29] Yü Sung-hua devoted
considerable attention to the question of Hebrew in Palestine. One
important aspect of the Jewish rebirth, he wrote, was the revival
of Hebrew and its use in education. The question of the Hebrew

language presented several major problems, however. Jews went to Palestine from many different countries where they spoke only the languages of those countries (although he seems surprised that most Jews understood German) and, therefore, had no previous knowledge of Hebrew. If Hebrew was to be used successfully in education, explained Yü, Jews must first be taught the language. An additional problem arose in relation to Arabic. Both English and Arabic were official languages in Palestine, but meanings of words or expressions in Hebrew did not always correspond to meanings in Arabic or English. As a result, there were frequent conflicts.[30]

In sum, the Zionist movement was said to have been a national renaissance movement *(min-tsu fu-hsing yün-tung)*, of political and cultural significance for the Jewish people. The renaissance aspect was described either as the renewal of the ancient culture or the creation of a new culture, in addition to the establishment of the practical goal of supporting a national reconstruction in the ancient homeland. That language played a vital role in this process was mentioned repeatedly. The references to the development and use of Hebrew in national and cultural reconstruction no doubt reflected Chinese writers' concern in using spoken Chinese.

At the same time, however, reference was not made to the enthusiastic experiments aimed at using the Hebrew language in prose and poetry. As will be shown later, since a number of Chinese writers considered Yiddish an excellent literary vehicle, they apparently never sorted out the difference between Hebrew and Yiddish and probably lacked the resources for doing so. Their understanding of Zionism was similarly superficial, and they tended to perceive it as a monolithic political-cultural movement which Zionism was not. Although they correctly understood Zionism's central stress on returning to the homeland, because Jews as a people could not and would not assimilate with other peoples, they did not acknowledge some of the real differences of opinion within the Zionist movement which were evident almost from its very beginning.

At its inception and early in the twentieth century, two directions were evident within the Zionist movement. For one, the goal was political, to be achieved by diplomatic negotiations, with primary concern for the safety of Jews. Quick and effective political solutions to the Jewish problem were sought. Although others by no means ignored the physical dangers threatening European Jews, the second direction tended to emphasize the crisis of Judaism and the need for spiritual and cultural revival. Settling the land, according to this view, was only a partial solution. The message of Zionism must also be addressed to the millions who will not return to Palestine. These two views, one politically oriented, the other concerned with Jewish spiritual and cultural life, never entirely coalesced. Indeed, both issues grew increasingly more complex as other ideological matters came to play a role in the Zionist formulation, and the environment itself in which Jews lived underwent change.[31] Especially significant in this latter regard was the growth and assertion of the Jewish community in America. When Louis D. Brandeis (1856-1941) spoke in 1915 of the "ideals of the Jewish renaissance,"[32] he meant not only the new self-respect of the colonists in Palestine, but also the pride of Jews anywhere in belonging to the Jewish people. This definition, however, was not accepted by all Zionists.

Chinese writers did not attempt to make an exhaustive study of Zionism; this was not their goal, nor did they have access to large quantities of source materials. Essentially, they reported on the current scene, bringing renaissance movements elsewhere to the attention of Chinese readers. As they saw it, the renaissance of oppressed peoples, including the Zionist renaissance, resembled their own in practice.

Black People's Renaissance

The problems of American blacks as an oppressed minority and their relationship to the African homeland as well as the recent emergence of great black writers and artists were topics of discussion. The information which Chinese writers had was remarkably detailed, but unfortunately there are no clues in the articles as to how they obtained this information. Ko Sui-ch'eng apparently did considerable research on currently held views on race, and he cited several theories held by Western authorities. At the same time, however, he deplored the fact that these authorities neglected Indians and blacks.[33]

In contrast to Jewish history, which was treated in some detail, scant attention was paid to the African background of Negroes. Instead, Chinese writers focused on the condition of slavery, the emancipation of slaves, the status of blacks in America prior to and after World War I, and the various movements launched to improve their condition. Chinese writers stated that the causes of slavery in America must be looked for within American society, its culture, laws, and economy. Although slavery was abolished, the unequal treatment of blacks has continued and for this reason a new abolition movement has appeared aimed at ending black class status.[34] That blacks were considered inferior to others was deplored. The goal of black emancipation movements in the twenties was to bring about a change in attitude. Lincoln may have freed the slaves, commented Yü K'an but social attitudes towards them have not changed. Because the black problem has become a social problem as well as a problem of social psychology, blacks were now demanding equality.[35] Some writers, like Ko Sui-ch'eng, realized that the black problem in America was first and foremost a social problem. He and others pointed to the large proportion of blacks to the white population and told their readers that social complexities grew with increasing numbers of different kinds of colored people.

World War I was seen as the turning point in black history. After 1924, immigration was restricted and this created labor shortages since a large percentage of American laborers came from Europe. The gap was filled by blacks who began to move from the southern to the northern states. Black rural agricultural workers changed their lifestyle and became urbanized industrial workers. During World War I, moreover, black soldiers joined the American army. Increased involvement in white society, both as workers and soldiers, led blacks to expect rights and privileges which were, however, not forthcoming at the end of the war. Bloody race riots were the result, concluded Ko.[36]

Since World War I, new personalities have emerged, transforming the black movement into one of the most important national movements which the world must recognize and approve. There were outstanding leaders and men of talent: writers like James Weldon Johnson, musicians like J. Rosamond Johnson (1873-1954), artists like Henry O. Tanner (1859-1937), and critics like W. E. B. DuBois, wrote Ko. The various congresses held and the movements founded all anticipated a renaissance (fu-hsing) in Africa. Certainly, one of the strongest movements was that of Marcus M. Garvey (1887-1940) and his Back-to-Africa national (min-tsu) movement. Ko Sui-ch'eng was optimistic, stating that

among black people there is no lack of able men,
and the future of the black people is bright. The
revolution is not yet finished and comrades still
must put forth effort; [if] the effort is skillfully
managed then white people's treatment of them
cannot be forever unequal.[37]

Others noted that even though blacks did not attend white
schools, they had their own schools, and 80 percent of the black
population was literate. However, white Americans opposed black
progress and there was much mutual hatred. Regarding prohibi-
tions of intermarriage in Virginia, for example, Yao Hsiung remarked with some surprise on the white belief that black blood
would destroy civilization. To him, this was incongrous with
American social reality, where whites and blacks had a common
language, a common religion, and lived side by side in the same
society.[38]

The Garvey movement was commented on at length by several
Chinese writers, who were highly optimistic regarding the movement's future. Marcus Garvey, they stated, had proven to white
society that blacks were not naturally inferior, and Garvey's Back-
to-Africa movement was the same as revolutionary movements elsewhere. It attempted to unite blacks throughout the world and
steadily gained strength. The aim was to return to the homeland
(ku-hsiang) in Africa.[39] According to Yü K'an, the foremost goal
of the Garvey movement was to bring about an African renaissance
(fu-hsing). Garvey's intention was to restore self-respect among
blacks, comparable to that which whites have. Until Garvey pro-
claimed the importance of black self-consciousness, there were not
sufficient elements within black society to stimulate such self-
respect. Black people trusted in Garvey, and their faith in him
was similar to the Indians' faith in Gandhi. Indeed, Garvey in
many ways resembled Gandhi, Yü concluded.

But in spite of the strength of this message and his popularity, not all blacks accepted Garvey's ideals, particularly the notion
that white culture (wen-hua) should be abandoned. "Ordinary
blacks," observed Yü K'an,

for the most part venerate white people, esteem-
ing themselves lightly. If only they were able
to change shape with the white man. Because of

Garvey's strong opposition to this view he offends
especially the ordinary person's hope of "integrat-
ing white and black people". . . .

Garvey, furthermore, was aware of the role which religion
played in black society. By resorting to religious imagery to convey his message, he had a powerful appeal. That Garvey was
imprisoned for fraud, which led to a rapid decline of his popularity,
was not especially disturbing to Yü K'an. Rather, he implied that
the black leader behind bars continued to exercise effective authority, and he cited Garvey's letter from the Atlanta Federal prison.[40]

In their descriptions, Chinese writers certainly touched on
most of the high points of the black American scene in the twenties.[41] These features, especially in regard to national self-
definition and the belief that energetic cultural leaders will bring
about a renaissance, are readily recognizable as New Culture aims.
In the black movements, whether as Harlem Renaissance or Back-
to-Africa, Chinese intellectuals of the twenties saw a correspon-
dence to and affirmation of their own renaissance. Similar to themselves, black cultural leaders, writers, artists, and publicists
established open dialogue and discourse in numerous publications.
And blacks conjured "the vision of a threshold of a new age of
black achievement," observed Nathan I. Huggins, whose views are
particularly relevant here. Although there were frequent quarrels,
disagreements, and often bitter antagonism, for the first time
blacks were heard by their own people and by others. Black intellectuals in Harlem—for that was where most of them were—conceived of themselves as both the creators of, and the actors in, a
rebirth of their people. This rebirth, they believed, would take
a variety of forms—national, political, cultural, and artistic—and
included in it the notion of the New Negro, freed from subservience.
Like the Chinese, black intellectuals considered their own efforts
as part of similar efforts elsewhere. Throughout the twenties,
theirs was a boundless optimism, and they felt that art and poetry
was the bridge that would span the gulf between the races.

Whether as image or reality, Africa played a role in the
blacks' attempt at self-definition and especially in their search for
a heritage. Although the Garvey movement was unequivocally dedicated to the political goal of liberating Africa and returning there
(thus being frequently referred to as "Black Zionism"), black
writers also expressed ambivalence in reference to Africa.

Culturally, the Harlem intellectuals were simply not Africans, and most knew it.

That blacks conceived of their efforts in a wider context was due not only to the imagined, romanticized, or actual African tie, or to a perception of a common spirit with others engaged in similar quests, but also to the Harlem setting in New York. The message of Garvey's Back-to-Africa movement, especially, seemed to be addressed to blacks everywhere. From Harlem, notes Huggins, Garvey "touched the hopes of hundreds of thousands of black people throughout the world. Garvey's coming to Harlem helped make it seem a capital for an international black race."

One further point deserves mention. It seems hardly accidental that Chinese writers chose to describe Jewish and black movements. Although they did not draw the parallel in their writings, some curious similarities are worth noting. There was a Jewish as well as a black diaspora. In both cases, some opted for assimilation —blacks searched for equality in an increasingly industrialized American society, and Jews wanted emancipation and to become a part of European society. But both also had a minority which suggested an alternative: return to the land of origin in the form of Zionism and Pan-Africanism. Together with attempts at self-definition and search for identity came intense cultural, political, and publicist activity. There were eloquent and creative men and women whose voices were heard beyond the confines of their immediate setting. In reaching out, Jews and blacks adopted similar techniques, and during the early years of the twentieth century international congresses and meetings proliferated. Inevitably, however, splits and schisms developed, thus invalidating further comparisons. [42]

The Harlem Renaissance may have ended as America's great depression deepened in the first part of the thirties. The concerns of the Zionist movement may have taken different forms as Jewish settlements struggled for survival in Palestine and the specter of mass persecution began to loom in Europe. However, as movements of minority peoples within hostile majority societies, and as movements whose initial aims were self-definition and cultural and political self-expression, they could not but attract the attention of Chinese commentators. The spirit of self-determination pollinated the world in the twenties, writes Huggins, [43] a world of which Chinese intellectuals considered themselves a part.

The Irish Literary Revival

The Irish were different. Neither return to the land nor
minority problems were issues. Together with Poles, blacks, and
Jews, however, they shared the drive for self-determination and a
common group memory demanding to be expressed in new cultural
and political forms. According to Chinese views, the Irish Literary
Revival was in every sense a renaissance movement. The goals of
the Literary Revival were part of Ireland's social and political movements in the late nineteenth and early twentieth century.

Materials on Irish history and literature, poetry and folktales
were apparently available, and both Cheng Chen-to and Mao Tun
made ample use of E. A. Boyd's *Ireland's Literary Renaissance*
(1916). The chapter on Irish drama in Frank W. Chandler's
Aspects of Modern Drama (1918) provided much of the background
for discussion on the emergence of modern Irish theatre.[44]

Descriptions of the Literary Revival pointed out that Irish
literature was different from British literature and that the Irish
were a unique people. According to Cheng Chen-to, the Irish
were a Celtic people with their own culture and their own scholarship. They had been unsuccessful in their frequent requests for
independence and freedom. A willful and fiery people, the Irish,
in spite of accepting Christianity, retained their ancient beliefs
in the supernatural. The nineteenth century in Ireland was marked
by the struggle for freedom and political independence. The Literary Revival began at the same time. In its initial stage, poetry
was written, and attempts were made at rediscovering the ancient
texts of the Gaelic and the pre-Christian tradition. The Celtic
Revival, as this was called, coincided with the Literary Revival
and both were related to Irish political movements. Cheng pointed
to the romantic quality in the poets' recall of the past as well as
the revolutionary fervor manifested in the 1916 Easter Rising.[45]
The subjugation of Ireland and the struggle for independence was
also described by Liu Pan-nung. For the past seven hundred
years, wrote Liu, Ireland has had revolutionary movements, the
most recent of which was the Sinn Fein movement. Now the struggle for independence had been joined by writers and poets.[46]

Elsewhere Chinese writers stated that the splendid culture
of the ancient Celts may be said to have returned, and the dream

of the poets of the Irish countryside was already partially realized.
Although the Irish people lost their independence seven hundred
years ago, they did not lose their spirit of peoplehood. Therefore,
both poets and scholars supported the present national movements
together with the Celtic movement. In Mao Tun's view, the Literary
Revival was furthermore important because it addressed itself to
people's emancipation. Although Ireland's new literature was pecu-
liarly Irish and expressed the Irish spirit, its concern with emancipation provided this literature with a universal context.[47]

Most writers pointed out that the renaissance quality of the
Literary Revival was due to Young Ireland, that is, the new Irish
writers' concern in their works with the lives of the common people
and the peasants. Several unique elements were said to have been
combined in the renaissance movement of the Irish. A newly formu-
lated nationalistic political movement opposed to the autonomy of
the English government in Ireland gave direction to incipient artistic and scholarly concerns. The latter, on the one hand, probed
into Ireland's pre-English past and attempted to revive Gaelic as
the language of the Irish as well as to bring back the ancient folk
traditions in that language. In addition, a group of new writers,
dubbed Young Ireland or the Anglo-Irish writers, using idiomatic
modern Irish and drawing on contemporary life, turned to folk
themes and created a new literature of great vitality and high artistic merit. In both endeavors—the antiquarian and the creative
—the nationalist impulse was a moving force.

The revival began in the 1890s. There is no agreement on
whether it had run its course in the twenties, thirties, or forties.
Like the Chinese Literary Revolution of the twenties, the initial
years of the revival were devoted both to an analysis of tradition
and to creative writing. Regarding the former, the nationalist
element was of major importance. Irish writers and scholars, comments Taylor, "showed a sensitive awareness of race and homeland
which led them to make repeated attempts at analysis of the Irish
mind. They were constantly looking for the Celtic element in the
writings of their associates and holding their contemporaries up to
judgement in the light of their Irish authenticity."[48]

Irishness, then, was the central ingredient in the Irish
Literary Revival. The same held true for the other renaissances.
For surely Jewishness was at the heart of Zionism, and blackness
was the major element in the Harlem Renaissance and the Back-to-

Africa movement. In this sense, each renaissance was particular
and advertised the provincialism of its authors and participants.
Provincialism, however, was not a consideration. Asserting particularity was a means of establishing identity, national or ethnic.
The search for identity was an element common to all of these
renaissances, and the medium used in this search was both political
and artistic. Possibly, as Huggins argues, this particularity of
artistic expression, so very necessary for establishing identity,
sets up limitations for good art. Is a particular art significant only
as provincial art, significant of itself, or is it possible to pass
through the province "into the world at large"?[49] Where is the
universal relevance of particular art?

The Chinese perception of the renaissances and the literature
produced in their course is in this regard uniquely interesting.
Chinese writers were not troubled by possible limitations in their
own New Culture and Literary Revolution, nor did they consider
limiting factors a problem in the renaissance of others. On the
contrary, they argued that as people generate a renaissance, the
world takes note of it. When writers of a particular people produce
outstanding literature, the world acknowledges it and such literature is seen as universally relevant. Mao Tun pointed out that in
nineteenth-century Europe neither Poles nor Jews had countries.
But after they developed new ideas, the world perforce recognized
their existence. Writers emerged who portrayed their people's
lives and thoughts, bringing them to the attention of the world.[50]
Particular renaissances of various peoples who formerly had no
hope, like the Irish, Poles, Jews, or Hungarians, when joined with
literary creativity, catapulted those peoples into the world arena.[51]
And Jewish or Irish writers, although writing of their own condition as well as about their own people's lives and experiences, have
had worldwide impact and influence.[52] Apparently, Chinese intellectuals did not consider particular renaissances with their specific
literatures either limited or provincial. On the contrary, entrance
to the world at large was via the province. As a consequence, they
also did not regard their own efforts as an isolated expression, nor
were the efforts of others remote. Writers were urged to take their
cue from oppressed peoples' literature in attempting to portray their
own world. Chinese writers can create, it was affirmed, universally relevant art.

Oppressed peoples' renaissances were further significant for
focusing attention on common people and peasants, whose lives were

considered universally relevant. Chinese writers did not suggest that Irish and Chinese peasants were alike, but they did suggest that all simple folk participate in a substratum of existence and, therefore, their lives can be understood by others. This is especially true when, as some Polish writers were said to have done, the common people were included as full-fledged partners in the national struggle. The importance of literature in this respect was that it "reflected life" or expressed "the complexity of life," was concerned with social realities, and was not an art form for its own sake. "I feel," wrote Mao Tun, "that literature which is representative of the life of society is true literature, and is literature which has a relationship to human beings. . . ."[53] A society within which individual human beings exist provides the universal context in all its particular variety. Chou Tso-jen's "human literature," and popular literature (ping-min ti wen-hsüeh), defined as realistic literature, expressed a similar idea. A literature of realism dealt precisely with the everyday lives of everyday people. The importance of oppressed peoples' literature, as Chinese writers saw it, was that the use of the literary technique of realism coincided with wider intellectual and political currents. Often Chinese writers tended to consider realism more than an artistic device, for changes in art, it was stated, would induce changes in other areas.[54]

A final aspect of universality and particularity in renaissance movements was that oppressed peoples' literature searched for traditional roots. According to Chinese writers, although a renaissance asserted the new, this did not imply breaking with the past. Had this been so, the quest for national identity would have been meaningless, for all such quests must necessarily be anchored in some kind of shared history. Memories held in common by the group, often as idealization, are both a bond for the present and the link to the future. Therefore, when Chinese writers pointed to the way blacks, Irish, or Jews handled tradition, they expressed their own concern of how to relate New Culture and Literary Revolution to China's tradition. In this respect, they shared with the Yiddish writers of the late nineteenth century a special awareness of the turning point in their histories. China would never be the same after May Fourth, just as Jewish Eastern European society had irrevocably changed after making contact with European culture. But precisely for this reason, the past and all it implied could not be consigned to oblivion. Thus, the new writers of Yiddish literature were said to have made available once more the Jewish national heritage. Irish writers similarly returned in their works to Irish tradition and traditional beliefs, and W. B. Yeats, for example,

made rich use of his people's ancient myths. The powerful historical novels of the Polish writer Henryk Sienkiewicz were still another
example. By means of historical fiction, Polish writers rediscovered
the riches of their national past.[55]

Implied in the Chinese writers' discussion is, of course, the
idea that the authors of oppressed peoples' literature were uniquely
aware of their past and were self-consciously engaged in creating
works that linked past and present. Clearly, therefore, Chinese
writers were not content to merely present general outlines of oppressed peoples and their literature; they also wanted to introduce
their readers to the men and women who wrote this literature. Who
were the outstanding writers? Whence their sensitivity to the times
and their artistic skills? The following section will describe some
of the views concerning authors of oppressed peoples' literature.

Writers Among Oppressed Peoples
Who Created Renaissances

The October 1921 issue of *Short Story Monthly,* which introduced examples of oppressed peoples' literature, gave one of the
reasons for doing so in the following words:

> A people's literature manifests the nature of that
> people. It is the background of their history,
> the background of their society and their various
> writings of the popular ideas of their time! If
> we want to explain a people's true inner feelings
> we can do so by reading their literary works. . . .[56]

The historical and social background as well as the overriding
idea in oppressed peoples' literature was the search for freedom,
independence, and peoplehood. Literary figures were thought to
be deeply involved in these issues, although their search might
have taken various directions.

Władisław Reymont and Henryk Sienkiewicz were the most
frequently discussed among Polish writers. Reymont, the writer
of peasants, was described as a peasant himself, who as a youth
was poverty-stricken. His works neither idealized nor degraded the
peasants, and Reymont described their hardships and suffering as
well as their human vitality. In showing the transformation of the

Polish soul from one of patient suffering to readiness for battle,
Reymont was, however, not a propagandist but a consummate artist,
wrote Hu Yü-chih. According to Fan Chung-yün, Reymont was a
neo-naturalist *(hsin tz'u-jan)*, although Fan did not explain precisely what he meant by this. Nor it is clear why he considered
Reymont superior to Sienkiewicz in his overall attitude to life.[57]

Sienkiewicz had more translations into Chinese than any other
Polish author, and his works were fairly widely read either in
English or Chinese translation, but there were only several brief
biographical notices. Mao Tun, who deeply admired the Polish
author's historical novels (although reading them required much
patience, he wrote), felt that Sienkiewicz led all others in creating
a new national literature. His prominence as an author was due
not only to his extraordinary productivity, nor even to his winning
the Nobel Prize in 1905; Sienkiewicz was truly great, wrote Mao Tun,
because he combined objectivity with subjective elements in his
work, skillfully tempering realism with romanticism. The statement
reflected Mao Tun's view that mere objective observation could
easily become one-sided description, and hence the importance of
romanticism. There was, furthermore, Sienkiewicz's love of man-
kind and his belief that love was the basis of literature. According
to Mao Tun, Sienkiewicz could be compared to Tolstoy, even though
their notions on Christian morality might have been different.[58]

That Polish writers needed to be judged on other aspects in
addition to their artistic merit was obvious to Chinese critics. Although the subtleties and complexities of Polish nationalism must
have remained hidden from them, there is no doubt that they recognized it as a motivating artistic force. A recent critic pointed out
that the strength of Polish nationalism was manifested not only in
the content but also in the language of literature. The literature
of a subjugated people, wrote Mrosik, could only exist by developing a type of dual language. In order to keep the national thought
alive, this literature had to exist under the eyes of the conqueror.
The enemy had to remain unsuspecting, but the friend had to recognize the thought immediately.[59]

National emancipation also informed Irish literature. The
three major writers who were repeatedly discussed were W. B.
Yeats, Lady Gregory, and J. M. Synge. It is they who, according
to Mao Tun, represented a countercurrent in modern literature.
Instead of tending toward universality, these writers drew on their

country's own history and dealt with their people's special character.[60] Drama was one of their most important modes of expression,
and they developed a people's theater which was not concerned with
making profit. Their plays were real plays, wrote Mao Tun; they
dealt not only with social problems or political reform, but addressed
themselves to what was within human life.[61] Another comment
pointed to recent Irish drama as a drama that explored questions
of human nature, new and old ways of thinking, and the clashes
between the two. The new feeling for national culture was expressed
by dramas of contemporary peasant life, of which Synge was one of
its greatest exponents. His plays, noted the Chinese critic, described individual personalities and unique national customs. Synge
portrayed his characters as natural and practical people; he was
sympathetic toward their faith, work, and ways of thinking.[62]

W. B. Yeats, the 1923 Nobel Prize winner, received considerable attention. But Yeats, wrote Wang T'ung-chao, was not easily
dealt with. His ideas were strange and different and were hard to
understand. They were rooted in the past and in the people's traditions, and at the same time expressed his hopes and feelings for
Ireland. Therefore, if one understood Yeats's Celtic background,
the mystic and occult elements in his works would also be clearer.
According to Wang, it was the philosophic content that was important. "I believe," he wrote, "that a philosopher has not necessarily a poet's way of thinking, but a poet certainly has a philosopher's way of looking at things." Yeats's philosophy can be
described simply as "criticism of life" (sheng-ming ti p'i-p'ing).[63]

Cheng Chen-to pointed out that Yeats gave new vitality to
Irish literature. He freed Irish literature from its dependence on
England and English literary criticism. That Ireland today had a
national literature which was not English literature was due primarily to Yeats's efforts, wrote Cheng. Yeats, furthermore, was
the most powerful figure in the Irish Literary Revival. Foreign
influences were noticeable in his earliest works, thought Cheng,
but he soon emerged as a purely Irish poet writing about Irish
tradition and the beliefs and customs of the masses. Although in
his later works symbolism predominated, the poetry of the 1890s
had as their subject peasants and villages.[64]

The Literary Revival was marked by "poets of the countryside." Among them was A. E. (George W. Russell), who described
the way in which people lived and the way they made their living.

He and others spoke of the countryside's richness and strange-
ness.[65] In sum, Polish and Irish writers searched their national
past in order to express contemporary concerns. The subjects of
their works were the common people, peasants, and the countryside. Nationalism and social issues were the twin motivations of
writers.

That these writers who turned to the countryside and peasants for their materials were of comparatively affluent background
was not stressed, although Reymont's humble origin invited considerable admiration. Hu Yü-chih, for one, mused that China was an
oppressed and agricultural nation like Poland; and yet, among millions of peasants, there was not one who wrote about the lives and
souls of Chinese peasants.[66] However, the question of a writer's
social background and standing in relationship to his work was to
become an issue only after 1949.

Although the poets of the Harlem Renaissance were known
and their poetry, such as that of Langston Hughes, was translated,
biographical data and critical discussions were scarce. Paul
Laurence Dunbar was praised for initiating new directions in black
poetry and for abandoning religious themes. Apparently more was
known about Claude McKay. He was a worker who hailed from
Jamaica, commented Chao Ching-shen. As a writer, he was neither
contrite nor did he plead with God for freedom. McKay was a
revolutionary.[67]

Among Jewish writers, however, even authors like David
Frischman (1886-1922) and Leo Kobrin (1873-1946), whose works
were not translated into Chinese, received biographical notices.[68]
Attention was paid to the authors' origins and the way they came
to be writers of literature in Yiddish. In an article translated from
Japanese, David Pinski was admired for his works on the oppressed
and his exceptional sympathy for the impoverished. Pinsky wept,
stated the author, over human weakness and over his own impotence
to relieve the distress of the soul.[69] According to Mao Tun, Y. L.
Peretz and Shalom Aleichem were unsurpassed in Yiddish literature.
Peretz was not only a superb short story writer, but his use of the
method of realism was unequalled as well. These and other writers
contributed to their people's renaissance because they discarded
Hebrew, the dead and old literary language (wen-yen), and sub-
stituted for it the living spoken language, Yiddish, wrote Mao Tun.
The use of Yiddish for literary purposes was a revolution of the

written language *(wen-tzu ke-ming),* and it was the means by
which modern Jews could be exposed to the racial wisdom of their
brothers.[70]

Most Chinese comments stressed innovation in the use of language among the creators of the renaissance. Black writers, like
Dunbar and McKay, were important because they wrote dialect
poetry. Among Irish writers there was Synge who introduced the
spoken peasant language into literature.[71]

To Cheng Chen-to or Mao Tun, the question of language was
crucial, since obviously the writing of new literature would become
possible only with new uses of language, as was pointed out earlier.
Their own goals were no doubt reinforced when they realized that
others also had to resort to innovations in the use of language.
Mao Tun and Cheng Chen-to's sensitive awareness of the problem
of language in addition to content is admirable. They failed, however, to perceive some major subtleties of language innovation
elsewhere. In the case of Ireland, the differences between Gaelic,
English, and modern Irish or Anglo-Irish were never sorted out.
Thus Chinese writers failed to perceive the importance to the
Literary Revival of the champions of Gaelic who opposed "anglici-
zation" and fought passionately to preserve Irish identity and culture. Nor was black dialect poetry seen as the mixed blessing it
was. James Weldon Johnson, one of the major Harlem Renaissance
poets, for example, felt that dialect poetry, rather than serving
the black cause, helped promote the stereotype.[72] Yiddish was
still more problematic. In spite of having translated an essay on
Hebrew poetry by T. Shipley which clearly spoke of a Hebrew
literary restoration *(fu-huo),*[73] Mao Tun never corrected the impres-
sion that Yiddish replaced Hebrew. Nor did he write at any other
time that Hebrew was assuming a new literary significance during
this period.

Chinese intellectuals, like Irish or Harlem intellectuals, were
supremely conscious of their role and purpose. By attempting to
understand and describe the renaissances elsewhere, they were
asserting the particularity of their own and other renaissances.
Together with the particularity of renewal, however, was also the
notion of the universality of renewal. Renewal was the betterment
of the human condition everywhere. One of the truly distinguish-
ing marks of the Chinese renaissance was that while it lasted, its
actors and creators bent their ears closely to listen to voices from

afar. And the voices they heard were those of inspired poets and writers who expressed joyful or pained awareness of belonging to a people or a nation. Because the New Culture movement was also an expression of nationalism, the Chinese keenly searched for similar expressions in other renaissances. To Chinese intellectuals, nationalism was more than a political phenomenon; it reinforced the particularity of renewal, and nationalism as cultural assertion—as identity—in no way contradicted the ideal of universal betterment.

III

TRANSLATIONS FROM OPPRESSED PEOPLES'
LITERATURE IN THE TWENTIES

Translating from foreign literature was a part of the Literary
Revolution, and the twenties were significant for extensive translation activity. Works from the great literary classics of the West
were translated, as were works from the literatures of oppressed
peoples. Although interest in practically all Western literature was
widespread, oppressed peoples' literary works, particularly of the
nineteenth century, attracted the attention of large numbers of
writers and translators. Whether as prose, poetry, or drama,
these works dealt with social and political concerns closely resem-
bling those expressed by Chinese intellectuals at the time. There
were the problems of nationalism and revolution; national identity
and freedom from foreign oppression; the apathy or stirring of the
masses; the plight of the peasant; and the beginnings of cultural
change and its implications. Here were descriptions of war and how
it affected the poor, and how the strong exploited the weak; here
also were stories and plays about the urban middle class and the
loneliness and alienation of city living.

Equally significant was the fact that Chinese translators and
critics respected, if not admired, the authors of such works. Nineteenth-century writers of oppressed peoples' literature, like Chinese
translators and critics, were deeply aware of their role as transmit-
ters or rejuvenators of their culture via the medium of literature.
They viewed their task as a historic one and their period as a historic turning point. They seldom doubted their influence on contemporary events. Nor did Chinese translators fail to appreciate the
artistic merits of these writers' works. The skillful fusion of humor
or satire with the often bitter tales of such masters as Sienkiewicz
and Shalom Aleichem was no doubt a major reason that so many of
both authors' works were translated into Chinese. The innovative
use of language, especially the lively spoken language of the

common people, as in, for example, the plays of John M. Synge, must have been equally appealing. Here, Literary Revolutionists had excellent examples of what they were trying to put into practice, namely, the use of the vernacular as a literary medium.

Not all of the works that were translated can be discussed here. For this reason, a number of representative examples have been chosen for summarizing in order to illustrate the variety of works that attracted the attention of writers and translators. A full listing of translated items by year of appearance can be found in Appendix A.

It must be emphasized that translations were prepared selectively and not at random.[1] This meant that in spite of the limited number of works of oppressed peoples' literature available to writers and translators, selections were made from these for materials to be translated. Whatever the specific criteria for selection, there were clearly certain types of works that were omitted. From Yiddish literature, for example, stories that dealt with anti-Semitism were not included. And the theme of romantic love was barely represented; the few items which were translated, moreover, stressed love's negative aspects. Thus, anti-Semitism and fulfillment in love were apparently themes not considered, although works with such themes appeared in anthologies or collections from which other works were chosen. Appendix B is a partial listing of works (not all the translations could be traced to their sources) from which translations were prepared.

The translated stories, plays, and poems fit into specific categories of themes which reveal to some extent the criteria for selection. The largest category is of themes that deal with social and political issues. Included in this category are works on social injustice, politics, oppression, war, exile, peasants, and problems of tradition and religion in societies that were beginning to undergo change. A second category deals broadly with reflections on life and philosophical issues, such as the meaning of existence, faith, goodness, personal isolation, and love as suffering. To this category also belong stories that utilize humor as a technique for dealling with deeper questions of human existence. A third category consists of translations of folktales and, though small, is significant for reflecting the incipient interest among Chinese intellectuals regarding their folk heritage.

Social and Political Issues

By far the largest number of works translated was concerned with social criticism. The reasons are obvious. The poverty-stricken masses had neither the means of redressing their grievances nor of improving their lot. Writers who took up their cause showed in sparse but powerful language the extent of human brutalization due to oppression and exploitation. The indifference of the rich and powerful was often emphasized.

Among Yiddish writers, David Pinski denounced in ringing tones social injustice and oppression. His one-act play, *The Cripples*, [34]* translated by Hu Yü-chih, describes the dehumanization of three crippled beggars. As they fight among themselves for a spot at the church entrance, it is apparent that they are incapable of compassion even for one another. But Pinski condemns society, not the men. One of the cripples is a disabled worker, another an incapacitated soldier. The church sexton, who represents the exploiting establishment, realizes the possibility of easy profit and informs the unfortunates that whoever gains the coveted spot will have to pay rent. Pinski's "Tale of a Hungry Man" [53] similarly indicts an indifferent society. A starving man who at first lashes out at society finally attacks a policeman and is jailed. But instead of bowing to fate, he defies all and commits suicide in his cell. Although society robbed him of human dignity in life, his death at least is in his own hands.

Dehumanization that grows out of oppression is the major theme in Reymont's "The Trial." [21] Unlike Pinski who points accusingly at society in general, Reymont in this story blames the corrupt bureaucratic establishment. A group of villagers, aware that neither police nor justice will protect them, brutally lynch a pair of petty thieves. A significant aspect of both "The Trial" and Pinski's "Tale" is that neither portrays passive acceptance. Here is active resistance, not ennobling to be sure, but possibly not as demeaning as suffering at the hand of the oppressor. Żeromski, in "Twilight," [8] holds corrupt landowners responsible for brutalizing the peasants. A landless peasant who engaged in petty graft loses his job. He and his wife now earn their livelihood by digging out a swampy marsh. He is a moody and crude type with no thought

*Bracketed numbers refer to the chronological listing of translated works in Appendix A.

for the baby that was left unattended in the cottage. His wife is torn between a mother's concern and fear of her husband's blows.

Poverty perverts and distorts human feelings; it makes for callousness. Brutal husbands are matched by indifferent wives. Tseng Hsü-pai's translation of Sholom Asch's "Abandoned" [63] is a bitterly humorous tale about a thief whose wife absconded with the loot, leaving him alone with a hungry infant. When he fails to rid himself of the crying baby, the father-thief accepts his responsibility and goes out to beg for milk.

The theme of social criticism was muted in translations from Irish literature. It appeared strongly only in the thirties, when twentieth-century Irish authors began to be translated. In some of Lady Gregory's plays, social criticism exists as an undercurrent while humorous twists and Irish nationalism are more conspicuous. In *The Rising of the Moon*, [6] a policeman—clearly representative of the English and their law—is to watch for an escaped Irish patriot. Although he recognizes the cleverly disguised revolutionary, he cannot bring himself to apprehend the man when the latter appeals to his Irish sentiments. The revolutionary's farewell to the policeman is, "You did me a good turn tonight. . . . Maybe, I'll be able to do as much for you when the small rise up and the big fall down. . . ." Open ridicule of British law is at its best in *Spreading the News*, [43] translated by Mao Tun. An officious magistrate and an incredibly stupid policeman help to concoct a muddled tale of murder and a runaway husband. Simple, gullible, though gossipy country folk are shown in juxtaposition to addled and officious representatives of the law.

The miseries of war and how they affect the poor and helpless found vivid expression in Polish and Yiddish literature. World War I and its perfected techniques of warfare deeply etched many a writer's creative genius. In "The Sowers" [54] by Reymont, spring has come to a village in a war zone. Inner, perhaps blind, compulsion makes the villagers leave their underground hovels to work the fields. Cannon fire kills many, but they continue to sow the seed. Two short plays by Pinski, both translated by Mao Tun, are close-ups of brutality and suffering in war. *Poland 1919* [33] describes a group of people trapped under bombardment in no-man's land. Pinski sarcastically exposes their shallow notions on politics, life, death, and God just before they die. *The Beautiful*

Nun [18] portrays the conduct of men in war who, no longer governed by human and religious values, attack a nun in church.

The translators' postscripts to "The Sowers" and *Poland 1919* might be briefly mentioned here because they referred the Chinese reader to additional dimensions in both. Regarding "The Sowers," Ku Te-lung commented that all Polish writers had the taxing job of writing about peasant life and the peasant movement. The reason was that Poland's revolutionary movement for independence was aimed not only at unifying Poland, but also at solving the peasant problem. Mao Tun saw in *Poland 1919* broad implications. Pinski more than mocked politics, religion, and poetry, wrote Mao Tun; he wanted to show that in the face of death, ideas lost their power and became meaningless.

Of the several stories that deal with political issues in a fictional setting, "Swallows and Butterflies Do Not Understand" [11] provides a good example. It describes how two youngsters inadvertently cross over the German border. When they are warned, the children begin to reflect on animals which move freely without care of borders. The boy's explanation is sadly ironical: human beings confined to boundaries supposedly have greater understanding than mere animals.

Exile and longing for the native soil were discussed by Sienkiewicz and A. Szymanski. Sienkiewicz's moving descriptions of self-exiled Poles in America and their peripheral existence in American society were based on his 1876-78 American journey. Szymanski wrote from personal experience; he had been sent to Siberia in 1878 for his part in the 1863 Polish uprising against Russia. In "Srul—from Lubartow" [25] a Pole and a Jew meet in Siberia. Far from home, in strange and unaccustomed surroundings, both pine for the native land. As exiles, Jew and Pole overcome their differences and unite in love and longing for the distant home. "A Pinch of Salt" [40] tells a different story. For their Christmas dinner, a group of exiles is joined by one who has spent three years among the remote Yakut peoples. All but the new arrival are in high spirits as they sit down to the feast. However, though his plate is heaped high, the newcomer will not eat. With tears in his eyes he explains that for three years he has not tasted salt.

50

From Irish and Polish literature there are a number of works
about peasant life in which social or political criticism is muted if
not altogether absent. In this group, Synge's plays are particularly significant. Unlike Lady Gregory's boisterous and often mis-
chievous countryfolk, Synge's peasants are individuals with personal aspirations and complex interpersonal relations. Like the
Polish peasants, they are wretchedly poor. But where the Polish
peasant struggles merely to survive, Synge's peasants search for
and sometimes find more satisfactory states of existence. Such is
the case with Nora Burke, a young and unfaithful wife, married to
an aging and dull man in *The Shadow of the Glen*. [62] Aware of
Nora's escapades, the husband pretends to be dead in order to
catch her red-handed. A passing tramp discovers the old man's
ruse. While Nora's lover discusses their impending marriage (now
that the old husband is supposedly dead), she begins to waver.
It seems no more than the exchange of an older for a younger and
equally predictable version of a man, she muses, and her humdrum
life will continue. After the "dead" husband jumps off the bed,
and the lover tries to escape, Nora leaves with the tramp for a
free and unpredictable life.

A somber note is sounded in "The Ploughman" [12] by
Gomulicki, where the peasant's relationship to the soil is explored.
The story describes an old and ailing peasant ploughing his field.
The peasant coughs and staggers but stubbornly carries on. When
questioned, the old man says that he must plow on even though he
will not see the harvest. His work is for those who come after him.

Gomulicki, like Reymont in "The Sowers," directs the reader's attention to a blind and compulsive attachment to the land. No
matter how disturbed their world or how feeble the body, peasants
are drawn as if by magic to work the earth. But the earth does
not bring happiness. It is a crushing burden. Irish peasant stories translated in the thirties made a similar point, as did those by
Chinese writers when they began to write about peasants and the
land.

The Yiddish writer Shalom Aleichem was a master of childrens'
stories in which he often described with uncommon sensitivity how
the world of adults was seen by the child. Adults are given to incomprehensible cruelty, feels the child; why butcher animals for
food? Why do boys kill birds for pleasure? Why is the cat unfairly
accused and punished for snatching food? These are the questions

the child asks in "Pity for the Living." [66] The only story that explicitly touches on the problem of anti-Semitism is also concerned with the lives of children. Feitel and Fedoka in "Passover in a Village" [67] are friends. One is Jewish and the other a gentile. It is the day of Passover eve, and the boys run off to the fields. They stay out longer than intended. Suddenly, sinister blood libel accusations are heard in the village. The story deals with the precariousness of Jewish existence and innocent children's friendship. The young boys are still blissfully unaware of their elders' dangerous prejudices and fears.

But stories with anti-Semitic content, like stories that deal specifically with Jewish existence, were generally avoided. An exception to the latter is "What is the Soul?" [44] by Peretz. It must have been difficult to translate, filled as it is with allusions to Jewish religion and practices as well as ideas that are not easily grasped outside the Jewish context. A boy persistently asks about the soul. His Hebrew teacher gives a religious explanation, but another teacher, a nonbeliever, says something else. A shy love for the nonbeliever's daughter leads the boy to put his question to her. She explains that when her mother was still alive, her father had called her his soul. The boy is satisfied and asks the girl to be his soul.

Among stories that deal with tradition and change, the best examples are "Winter" [9] by Asch and "In the Storm" [45] by Pinski. In the first, a matchmaker persuades a mother to break with tradition and marry off the younger daughter while the older remains at home and unmarried. The story describes the emotional turmoil this decision causes the mother and elder daughter. Single women were no more acceptable in traditional Jewish society than in traditional China, and girls from poor homes were usually married in accordance with age. The mother's decision, therefore, sealed the older girl's fate. The second story's sinister overtones are obvious. A Jewish girl has taken up with a nonbeliever, an "apostate," and is missing from home during a storm. Frightened by the violation of old ways, the mother curses the daughter. She then runs beyond the village, searching for her daugher, whom she finds struck dead by lightning.

Stories such as these carried a significant message. The persecuted, impoverished, and stagnating Jewish masses of Eastern Europe were beginning to confront changes which they had trouble

understanding and which threatened established customs and a way
of life. In their works, the great nineteenth-century Yiddish writers caught the moment of conflict between tradition and change. It
was a moment of fear and turmoil, and its often powerful portrayal
must have had a strong impact on Chinese translators and readers.

Translations in this category reflect upon human experience
in its infinite variety. But as portrayed there was little joy or love
in the lives of the common people; instead, these works describe
grinding poverty, indifference, and brutality. Glimmers of human
feelings were often submerged and barely expressed, and the unre-
mitting realism was only occasionally softened by bitter humor or
satire. To Chinese translators, this literature had social and political significance, as they indicated not only in general discussions,
but also in the occasional postscripts appended to the translations.
Chinese translators assumed an intrinsic relationship between literature and national consciousness, especially since this literature was
written in the spoken language of the people. The masses must be
confronted with their own condition, reasoned commentators, in order to develop the self-awareness of who they were. Self-awareness
would lead to common identity and the pursuit of common goals.
Social improvement was a part of political change and an ingredient
in movements for national independence. The movements of national
revolution therefore included social goals as defined by writers of
peasants and the common people. For New Culturists, then, this
literature was politically important,[2] a fact reflected in the works
chosen for translation and in their comments about them.

Reflections on Life

The second category of translated works, all of which in some
way thoughtfully take stock of life, is as large and diverse as the
previous category. However, in contrast to the robust and stark
realism of the first category, these works frequently appear senti-
mental, even insipid or contrived. This seems especially true for
those works that have an imaginary setting. Possibly they caught
the translators' fancy because of the way in which the authors
transposed philosophical questions to fictional settings. In works
that deal with the middle class, the search for values and meaning
in existence are major themes. The concerns of the middle class
were vastly different from those of peasants or poor people, but
they were no less real for Chinese translators who were themselves

middle class urbanites. In the group of works where the philosophical message is subordinate to the humorous presentation, this
technique might have attracted translators. On the whole, the
humor in these works is fairly sophisticated, as is the presentation
and development of the central problem of these stories.

For his story "Be Blessed," [24] Sienkiewicz chose an Indian
setting. Translated several times in the twenties and republished
in a number of journals and collections, the story deals with the
power of Lord Krishna, who causes the lotus, in the form of a
maiden, to reside in the heart of the poet Valmiki. There she
takes the attributes of happiness, compassion, beauty, and light.
Sienkiewicz's tale is intended to convey a message of human nobility
and goodness. Prus's "From the Legends of Ancient Egypt," [35]
on the other hand, tells a story of human scheming and the power
of evil. Ramses is about to die. His son Horus, who will inherit
the throne, plans to right the wrongs inflicted by Ramses. But
Horus succumbs to a poisonous spider's sting while Ramses miracu-
lously recovers. Was the grimness of Prus's message intended as a
warning to a generation of Chinese optimists who believed in the
power of truth and goodness? "Ormuzd and Ahriman," [170] by the
Yiddish author Peretz, is cast in the form of a conversation between
the author and a Persian. It too conveys a pessimistic view regarding the power of goodness. Among Persians there is a belief that
Ormuzd is a good divinity and Ahriman a wicked god and the spirit
of temptation. The Persian tells the author that belief in Ormuzd
is wavering because Ahriman is recently using new tricks. Instead
of destroying Ormuzd's good deeds, Ahriman corrupts them. Hence,
when Ormuzd gives a man courage, Ahriman adds more, causing
the man to become savage and adventurous. When Ormuzd gives
love, and love for the nation, Ahriman adds to it and the feeling of
love turns into chauvinism and jingoism. Both Peretz's and Prus's
stories have a political undercurrent which quite likely did not
escape the Chinese translators.

Yeats's play The Hour Glass [49] does not have a special setting but should be included here for its fanciful treatment of the
comparative value of rationalism and faith. A wise man who has
taught everyone empirical and rational knowledge is visited by an
angel. The angel announces his death and that neither heaven nor
purgatory is open to the wise man, he having denied both. However, if within the hour the wise man can find a believer, he will
be saved from eternal damnation. The wise man discovers that all

have become rationalists, except for the fool who has retained a childlike faith in the existence of angels. The problem here raised of rationalism versus faith was a widely debated issue among Chinese intellectuals in the first half of the twenties.[3]

Individual isolation and loneliness are a part of twentieth-century existence. Life in large cities and the attainment of degrees of comfort or affluence also led to reflections on the consequences of depersonalization and anonymity. Polish writers especially, perhaps because they tended to congregate in cosmopolitan Warsaw, expressed the dilemma of the individual's separateness. In "Shadows," [20] Prus compares individual existence to the life of a lamplighter. At dusk, the lamplighter moves like a shadow through the streets. He lights the street lamps and disappears. The author tells how he wanted to discover something about the man's life, but no one knew his background. Later, he is told that the lamplighter had died. So are we all, concluded Prus, silent like shadows. We travel through life, each with a small flame; we kindle a light, live unrecognized, toil without acknowledgement, and disappear like shadows.

Prus sounded a similar note in "Lichens of the World," [19] a story that emphasizes the helplessness of the individual when confronted by the passage of time, change, and the attempt to find meaning in history. The author is shown as looking at a stone overgrown with lichens. A botanist explains that lichens are like societies: they colonize and wage wars, although unlike people they have neither culture, souls, nor hearts. Looking at the lichens some years later, the stone suddenly seems to the author like a globe, with the lichens acting as continents that merge or separate. When asked whether the lichens represent human history, the botanist nods, but the author now presses him as to where the soul, the heart, and the culture of human history are.

Stories such as these, melancholy and pessimistic, were undoubtedly responsible for the far-from-enthusiastic evaluation that Chinese writers gave to more recent twentieth-century Polish literature. Shen Yü, for example, maintained that the earlier nationalism had given way to universalism in contemporary Polish literature. This universalism, he wrote, the attempt to link Poland to world culture, had not been conducive to artistic creativity, and Polish writers were not producing a representative literature.[4] This fiction, in part reminiscent of some of Yü Ta-fu's works,

certainly lacks the robustness of peasant stories and does not reflect the predominant optimism of May Fourth. However, one must
keep in mind that what to Chinese critics seemed unsavory cosmopolitanism was in Poland a revolutionary tendency, a demand for
freedom to create and an insistence that art not serve ideas.

Two more stories, the content of which is less concerned with
abstract ideas than with specific issues, should be mentioned. The
first is "My Aunt" [14] by Maria Konopnicka. In this story, a
young wife is to remain temporarily with an elderly maiden aunt.
The aunt is unwilling and expresses an unreasonable fear of children, suggesting that the wife might be having a baby while in her
home. At this point, the housekeeper announces that a foundling
has been left at the doorstep. Although the aunt insists on the
foundling's instant removal, she is persuaded to hold it for a moment.
Suddenly her behavior changes, mellows, and becomes maternal. It
would have been difficult to know why Chou Tso-jen chose to translate this story had he not appended a note of explanation. According to Chou, only Konopnicka as a woman writing about women
could show how a woman's emotions were subject to change. Only
a woman writer, he emphasized, could describe such matters with
certainty. Chou's interest in issues concerning women is well
known, yet the view that women writers deal best with women's
emotional life is remarkably contemporary and deserves to be
underscored.

The second story is "Sachem" [1] by Sienkiewicz and deals
with an American Indian rather than with Poland. Sienkiewicz's
1876-78 visit to America led him to write a series of letters with
observations on American life as well as a number of stories concerned with social injustice towards Poles and others. Most of
these were translated in the thirties, which I will discuss in the
next chapter. "Sachem" is one of the earliest translations from
Polish literature and is more complex than the stories discussed so
far. On the one hand, this is the portrayal of an Indian chief
whose tribal pride and human spirit were broken by the massacre
of his people and the loss of his lands. Humbled and speaking
German, he has become an entertainer to the very Germans who
destroyed his tribe. On the other hand, this is also a portrayal of
the German conquerors: their complacency, their philistinism, and
their cowardice when they fear revenge as the chief recounts the
end of his people. Sienkiewicz's vivid tales of physical and

psychological subjugation even in a remote setting carried a potent
message for the Chinese reader.

As mentioned earlier, romantic love stories that deal with
love's fulfillment were generally not translated, although they were
available in the anthologies from which other translations were prepared. There are, however, three stories on the theme of unhappy
love. "Does She Love Me?" [36] by Prus is a vignette of a young
man in love who, when trying to divine reciprocal feelings in the
young lady, sees her passing by on another man's arm. Unrequited
love also forms the content of "An Enduring Heart" [27] by Yeats.
Utilizing the storyteller's technique, a daughter asks her father to
tell her about love. He responds that no one ever marries the
woman he loves. As youths, continues the father, he and a friend
saw a young girl weeping at the docks. Nearby two men argued;
apparently the girl was being separated from her lover. Her brother was sending her to America. The father's friend decided to
leave on the same ship as the girl. Many years later, the father
also went to America and located the girl, now married, though not
to his friend. When asked about the friend, the woman wept un-
controllably. He never discovered why, although it must have had
something to do with their having been in love, concluded the
father.

Unhappy love is, furthermore, the theme of Pinski's play
Forgotten Souls, [7] with self-sacrifice as a secondary theme. (The
self-sacrificing sister was fairly common to the Yiddish stage.) A
woman is in love with a playwright who, in turn, loves her younger
sister. The woman's boarder, a cripple, is in love with her. Predictably, the woman does not fight to gain the playwright's love,
abdicating happiness to her younger sister, and in final desperation
settles for the crippled boarder.

The theme of love as suffering is universal and found an
eager Chinese audience, especially as developed in Goethe's classic
work *Die Leiden des Jungen Werther* (The sorrows of young
Werther), translated by Kuo Mo-jo in 1921. Possibly, the lack of
interest in love stories of oppressed peoples was due to the richer
and fuller treatment of the topic by major German, English, or
French writers. Certainly the three examples discussed are in no
way remarkable, and Pinski's play in particular seems fairly trite.

Among humorous stories, Sienkiewicz's "The Decision of Zeus" [56] is a masterpiece of satire. Apollo and Hermes, the latter also the guardian of merchants, admire Athens and Athenian women. Hermes remarks that they are also virtuous. Apollo, convinced that even the most virtuous of women cannot resist him, begs Hermes to select one suitable for advances. They find one and both gods conclude a wager. However, Apollo's nocturnal love song does not move the woman; cursed and rejected, Apollo desists, but he refuses to honor the wager. The gods ask for Zeus' judgement. Zeus decides in favor of Apollo since the woman, he says, was stupid and not virtuous.

Aside from the broadly humorous aspects of the story, its appeal to both translator and reader may very well have been due to Sienkiewicz's technique. Patrick Hanan points to the various forms of irony used by the Polish writer in his shorter works, which were adapted successfully by Lu Hsün. Although there certainly are examples of satire (no attempt is made here to differentiate between irony, satire, humor, and so forth) in traditional Chinese literature, "presentational irony conveyed by a more or less dramatized narrator standing outside the action"[5] as developed in particular by Sienkiewicz was different if not altogether new.

A similar technique, often in combination with pathos, was also used successfully by Lady Gregory in a number of her plays. Two excellent examples are her *The Jackdaw* [30] and *Hyacynth Halvey*. [13] In the first, a widowed shopkeeper is summoned to court for nonpayment of taxes. Her brother is willing to help, but does not want her to know. A comedy of errors ensues, in which an invented story, of a lonely Irishman in an African mine wishing to buy a crow, spreads like wildfire. Everyone envisions riches from crows sent off to distant Irishmen. In this play as well as in *Hyacynth Halvey*, there is the juxtaposition of village reality—narrow, confining, and poverty-stricken—with the fabricated reality of soaring peasant imagination. The two levels are skillfully exploited by Lady Gregory and are clearly conveyed to viewer or reader. In the second play, the character Hyacynth Halvey, newly arrived in the village, is a highly recommended subsanitary inspector. The Department of Agriculture, wanting to support the moral development of the rural population, plans to present a lecture on "The Building of Character." Meanwhile, gossip has transformed Hyacynth Halvey into a veritable saint, a reputation he does his best to destroy. But neither stealing a sheep nor robbing the church poor box can shake the villagers' belief in him. Hyacynth's deeds or misdeeds are further signs of his goodness. He is chosen as the most qualified person to lecture on character building.

This category of translated works is characterized by the great variety of issues raised and the various techniques used in discussing them. Questions of good and evil in human nature as well as the human propensity for excesses are among those examined. There is the insoluble dilemma of the individual's loneliness and isolation. There are stories and plays that investigate abstract ideas as well as the personal and emotional world of individual human beings. In distinction to the works that deal with social and political issues and which expose, deplore, or condemn various aspects of modern and modernizing society, these stories and plays are both more subtle and more complex. No doubt the major attraction of such works to Chinese translators was the often highly successful use of a fictional setting to convey philosophical notions.

Folktales

Interest in folktales was related to a general interest in folk tradition that grew and developed as the folklorist movement gathered momentum in the twenties. At first, the activities of Chinese folklorists were largely focused on the gathering of literary data. Although folklorists paid lip service to the slogan "to the people," they were more comfortable sifting data at their desks than in a spiritual confrontation with peasants. Leading Chinese intellectuals, such as Ku Chieh-kang or Chou Tso-jen, had much in common with Irish writers like Yeats, who had extolled the national heritage in the 1890s and championed "to the people" slogans, but who was more comfortable in Dublin. In fact, both the Irish Literary Revival and the Chinese folklorist movement were similar in exhorting the educated elite to search among the masses for true expressions of the national spirit.

The folklorist's interests also centered on Chinese history. Ku Chieh-kang's research into Chinese folklore, for example, was not divorced from his concern with China's past, and in his writings he attempted to show the continuities and integrative factors in Chinese history. Toward this end, he proposed new methods for investigating the past; he advocated the reinterpretation of the function of myth and legends that were operative in the formation of traditional concepts.[6]

The validity of the folklorists' arguments and the national concerns that informed their work need not concern us here. What is of interest is that their widely publicized efforts led others to a sensitive awareness of the interest in folklore elsewhere. The aim of folklore investigations in other parts of the world was thought to be similar to that of the Chinese. Thus, Mao Tun remarked that Irish writers in recent years had turned their backs on such questions as how to view life and the world and were looking for old beliefs in folktales.[7] And Hsi Ti in the introduction to his translation of Indian fables noted the subsurface meaning of fables as well as the fact that India was the birthplace of the fable. When fables appeared elsewhere, he suggested, they drew on the Indian tradition.[8]

Among works translated, four folktales retold by Yeats are noteworthy. They were first published in his book *The Celtic Twilight* (1893) and were translated by Wang T'ung-chao. The four tales are: "A Voice," which weaves together folk motifs and Christian ideas; "The Old Town," which tells of the ghosts of dead people who dwell in burned-out ruins of the town; "The Three O'Byrnes and the Evil Faeries," [50] the subject of which is a treasure that can be discovered only by the three O'Byrnes brothers, who, however, will die a horrible death the moment they find the treasure; and "Dreams That Have No Moral," [41] a wonderfully imaginative yarn reminiscent of the complex adventure stories popular in Chinese tradition. As explained in its prefatory remarks, the fourth story tells of times when actions had no consequences, when death was the occasion for renewed life, and when old dreams were sufficiently strong to throw off the burden of worldly cares. A childless queen is told to eat fish to increase her fertility. The cook tastes some while preparing it, and a dog and a horse eat the remains. During the following year, children are born to all, beginning their adventures where nothing is impossible. Cook, queen, dog, and horse continue to produce offspring "by the basketful," which are thrown out "by the shovelful."

Pinski's "Rabbi Akiba's Temptation" [32] is a less lighthearted tale which moralizes on excessive intolerance. Rabbi Akiba, a historic personality and one of the sages of Jewish tradition, has become something of a folk hero over the years. Uncommon experiences and deeds are attributed to him. This story tells of his disavowal of bodily pleasures. Having left his wife, Akiba travels through many lands and in each withstands numerous temptations. In one beautiful country, however, a naked woman beckons from a palm tree and Akiba climbs it. Halfway up he begins to weep, not because he succumbed to temptation but because of his former harsh intolerance.

Although translations from Indian literature are not included in this study, mention might be made of several dozen fables translated from the English of P. V. Ramaswami Raju's *Indian Fables* (1887).[9] They are short, charming tales of folk wisdom pronounced by foxes, owls, or frogs. Aside from folktales and fables, Chinese intellectuals and writers showed an interest in works of historical fiction. Such works, however, were not translated in the twenties, and the national epic poems of Mickiewicz, for example, found their way into Chinese only after 1949. Availability was apparently not the issue, because Mao Tun mentioned reading Sienkiewicz's historical novels, and finding them exciting literary materials.[10] Possibly their excessive length deterred translators. The message of national identity and assertion could be found elsewhere.

How faithful were the Chinese versions to either the translated or the original versions of these stories and plays? How did Chinese translators solve the problem of translating specific terms? How did they make intelligible religious and other practices that were foreign to Chinese readers? It should be emphasized that, generally speaking, the translations are readable, clear, and lively, and they closely follow the versions from which they were translated. Where there is a real difference between the Chinese and the original work, the cause can usually be attributed to the intermediate translation. Nonetheless, Chinese translators did encounter difficulties with specific terms. Often such terms were merely transliterated, and it was up to the reader to figure out the meaning. Sometimes explanatory footnotes were used; and if a work was heavily laced with colloquialisms, translators frequently tried to find more or less successful equivalents.

A few examples may suffice. One way of handling terms that defied translation was to transliterate them, sometimes adding the English equivalent or providing explanatory footnotes. Thus, the

Hebrew term *Torah* appears as *tu-la* without further explanation, or together with the statement that it refers to the Five Books of Moses. On the other hand, *ḥasid* (member of a pious Jewish sect), rendered in English in its Yiddish pronunciation of *ḥusid*, was transliterated as *hu-shi-ti* without clarification. *Kaddish,* the Jewish prayer for the dead, was not transliterated but translated as hymns *(tsan-mei-shih)* without further explanation. Phylacteries that are used in daily prayer by pious Jews were translated correctly as *ching-hsia* or scripture box, and their use was explained in a footnote. The Chinese equivalents found for colloquialisms or proverbs were often ingenious. *Shlemazl* (a person who never succeeds) became *tao-mei-chia huo* in Chinese, and "you blackguard" appeared as *ni chien-jen.* The Chinese proverb *ssu-sheng yu ming-ah* (death and life are caused by fate) took the place of "Blessed be He who gives, and He who takes." Someone who drank until "he made a beast of himself" simply drank until he was dead drunk *(ho-le i-ko lan-tsui).* A variety of terms were used for synagogue and church, such as *hui-t'ang, yu-t'ai li-pai t'ang,* or *ssu,* and God might be *shang-ti, shen,* or *lao-t'ien-yeh.*

In conclusion, the liveliest and most intelligible translations appear to be those that took liberties with the original text. Whenever translations did not attempt to be literal, and when they utilized Chinese equivalents as approximations, the translators more clearly conveyed the intent of the original. Whenever translators tried to be literal and faithful to the text, however, the result seems stilted, if not obscure. Therefore, the more sinified the translations and the more use of Chinese imagery, the more successfully did the translation preserve or highlight the intention and meaning of the original.

Two further considerations may be suggested in this connection. One is that a sinified translation does not imply a paraphrase of the original, such as that, for example, produced by Lin Shu at the beginning of the twentieth century. Rather, this kind of translation demanded that the translator be as fully conversant as possible with the materials to be translated. Involved here was the intelligent understanding of literary works, and no doubt supplementary reading and research were also required. In short, translating from oppressed peoples' literary works further supports the assumption stated earlier, namely, that translating was an intellectual as well as a literary activity. The second consideration involves uses of language. Because the works of oppressed people were for the most part written in lively everyday sppech and were interspersed with colloquial expressions, translators could freely experiment with Chinese colloquialisms and vernacular usage. Translating, therefore, was an excellent opportunity for developing the spoken language as a literary tool. Provided with stimulating content, Chinese writers could concentrate on forging a new language for literature.

IV

THE CHANGING IMAGE IN THE THIRTIES

In the twenties, translations from oppressed peoples' literature and discussions about this literature formed a strand in the New Culture and New Literature movements. The emphasis on nineteenth-century writers whose concerns were with national revolution and national identity supported the aims of Chinese intellectuals in the twenties. When at the end of the twenties the Chinese literary and intellectual scene underwent drastic change, and political exigencies imposed new demands that led to changing concerns, views on oppressed peoples and their literary works underwent change too. Translation activity continued, but fewer works were translated. And in addition to the ongoing interest in nineteenth-century writers, more recent writers and their works now also received attention. Aside from national revolution, the condition of oppression in the thirties was also related to social revolution and imperialism.

The increasing political and intellectual polarization in China after 1927, and especially after the establishment of the Nanking regime in 1928, affected the literary scene. Writers in the left-wing literary movement struggled for self-definition while developing at the same time a new literary orientation. Their voices were heard in a variety of more or less short-lived literary publications. The most important of these was the influential *Wen-hsüeh* [Literature], which appeared from 1933 to 1937 after the demise of *Short Story Monthly* in 1932. Non-leftist writers and intellectuals similarly attempted to define the direction and content of literary creativity in journals that were not necessarily any more stable than those of the left. Possibly the most important group of non-leftist writers was part of the Crescent Moon Society (*Hsin Yüeh*), which published its journal *Hsin yüeh yüeh-k'an* [The crescent moon monthly] from 1928 to 1933. Generally speaking, while the left attempted to evolve a mass line, meaning that they wanted to write for and about the masses, others, like the Crescent Moon group, espoused an undisguised elitism.[1] These contrary tendencies were apparent in the literary works of both groups as well as in the works chosen for translation by each. Thus, translations in *The Crescent Moon Monthly* were taken predominantly from Western literary classics, and not a single translation of oppressed peoples' literature appeared in its pages. On the other hand, left-wing journals, such as *Literature*, *Shih-chieh tsa-chih* [World journal], and *I-wen* [Translations], published oppressed peoples' literature from time to time. Moreover, like its predecessor *Short Story Monthly*, *Literature* devoted a special issue in 1934 to the works of oppressed peoples. During the thirties, then, interest in oppressed peoples and their works was professed primarily by writers with a leftist orientation, whose choices of works to translate frequently reflected their political convictions. In addition to this polarization of writers, notions of what constituted weakness and oppression also underwent change. In the thirties, the image of oppressed peoples underwent gradual transformation in the media, although this transformation was not evident in the literary discussions.

The outbreak of war in July 1937 dealt a major blow to literary and journalistic activities, which were concentrated in such major cities as Shanghai, Peking, and Tientsin. When, after the initial disorientation, publishing resumed in China's hinterland, interest in oppressed peoples' literature had for all practical purposes disappeared, and any sort of systematic translation activity apparently ceased during World War II and the 1946-49 Civil War which followed.[2]

Oppressed Peoples and Imperialism

When writing about oppressed peoples, Chinese commentators in the thirties concluded that there were varieties of oppression, and more specific definitions needed to be established. Thus, Hu Yü-chih proposed three different categories of oppressed people: (1) oppressed peoples *(pei ya-p'o min-ts'u)* who are under partial colonial and white domination; (2) minorities who are neither politically independent nor assimilated by the peoples among whom they live; and (3) small and politically independent countries that have emerged after World War I, but that cannot assert themselves culturally and economically because of big power oppresssion. The three categories may be different, but their common problem was

that they cannot develop freely, wrote Hu.[3] Another writer stipu-
lated five categories. In addition to Hu's three, he included abori-
gines such as Eskimos and American Indians and tributary (shu)
peoples like Albanians, Bhutanese, and Nepalese. In spite of their
differences, he wrote, these five shared a search for emancipation,
and their nationalist movements (min-tsu yün-tung) were revolutionary in opposing imperialist oppression.[4]

The cause of oppression was imperialism and the root of revolution was the attempt to throw off the imperialist yoke. The Irish
have always reluctantly submitted to British imperialism, and thus
there have been innumerable rebellions. In this regard, Britain's
imperial system was seen to be faced with mounting problems from
the independence movements in the colonies. In India and Ireland,
the independence movements agitated for political self-determination,
wrote Yang Jui-ling. While India was economically important,
Ireland's significance within the colonial system was political. According to Yang, the Irish movement was already too powerful for
the parent country (wei-ta-pu-tiao, literally "the tail is too big
to wag"). Cheng Chang was less optimistic and felt that Irish
strength was brittle. British imperialist oppression was severe,
he wrote, and the Irish independence movement had made no head-
way. All concurred, however, that the Irish desire for independence was strong and that a peaceful solution did not suggest
itself, especially because the Irish increasingly demanded the
world's attention.[5]

It was frequently pointed out that the Jews were dispersed
among all the nations. They were always persecuted, most recently
in fascist Germany, and because of these persecutions they developed either secret organizations, like Freemasonry, or public
organizations, like Zionism. Persecution had also led to the emergence of famous revolutionaries like Marx. And what was the
future of the Jews, asked the writer. "Ever since the Jews became
an international people, the solution of the Jewish problem is syno-
nymous with the solution of the international problem. . . ."[6] Although Chinese writers took note of growing German anti-Semitism
(p'ai-yu), anti-Semitic as well as sympathetic statements were
frequently combined, as in the abovementioned example of Freemasonry being equated with Zionism. Elsewhere a similar combination was made, when American Jews were said to own two-thirds of
America's gold. No prejudice was intended here, because the
author went on to say that the world was drifting toward anti-

Semitism, and yet neither poor nor rich Jews were willing to return
to their homeland in Palestine.[7]

The question of imperialism was more important than nationality. While discussing the Jews' desire to establish a national
state in Palestine, Wu Ch'ing-yu concluded that Jews had none of
the characteristics of a nationality. Nonetheless, this was irrele-
vant, because wherever they were, Jews unanimously opposed
imperialism.[8]

Thus, anti-imperialism, and not national self-awareness, was
the common feature of oppressed peoples. For China of the thirties,
increasingly confronted with the threat of Japanese imperialism,
this was a clear and obvious message—a message, moreover, that
was further highlighted by the condition of America's black population. Tsou T'ao-fen (1895-1944), journalist and editor of the
popular journal Sheng-huo [Life], traveled in America in 1935.
There he observed that blacks were like "a people without a country." They had neither territory nor sovereign rights and their
lives were miserable. Significantly, Tsou compared the condition
of blacks with that of China's masses, who were no better off. The
Chinese masses were threatened by Japanese imperialism with loss
of territory and sovereign rights—America's blacks were a symbol
of the Chinese people's fate.[9]

But what about literature? May Fourth intellectuals had
argued that writers of oppressed peoples created great literary
works in response to and as a rejection of their condition. Several
Chinese writers of the thirties made a similar claim. In their descriptions of these peoples' oppressed state, they asserted that
their literature, art, and scholarship always contained ingredients
of anti-imperialism and opposition to domination. Rather than cultural oppression and national assertion, literature as a tool in the
fight against imperialism was underscored in these general accounts.

Views on Writers and Their Works

Discussions of individual writers and their works did not
have the critical acumen they had in the twenties. The accounts,
often brief "fillers," continued to reveal a better acquaintance with
nineteenth-century writers than with those of the twentieth
century. In either case, however, critics rarely attempted to

convey a systematically compiled body of information. Whereas in general accounts oppressed status was related to imperialism, the notices on writers and their works did not stress this point.

In discussing black writers, Sheng Ch'eng seems to have gathered his impressions of recent developments on the American black literary scene in Europe. His informants, whom he described as colored people from America, Africa, and Asia, led him to the optimistic conclusion that the future no longer belonged to white men but to the younger societies, specifically the black people. The time when blacks wanted to assimilate culturally with their white world was past, he wrote. New black poets did not model themselves on Western literary masters, but dealt in their works with their own affairs and their own emotions. One of the most powerful new writers among black poets was Claude McKay, who advocated the writing of a militant literature. Sheng cited McKay as having said that "from a historic perspective, defeated countries and peoples who were compelled to submit have assimilationist tendencies and the culture of defeated countries. This is a slave culture and is not culture conscious of itself!" Aside from McKay, there were writers like Countee Cullen and Langston Hughes, whose works revealed self-knowledge and self-consciousness.[10]

It was in fact Langston Hughes who, during his brief July 1933 visit to Shanghai, introduced Chinese writers to McKay's works. Hughes was welcomed by "Shanghai's literary world,"[11] including Lu Hsün, and mentioned meeting the young Chinese man who was translating his novel *Not Without Laughter*.[12] It was not possible to ascertain whether this novel was ever published in Chinese translation. Hughes apparently also brought Walter White's works to the Shanghai writers' attention, and White was mentioned as a person who devoted himself to the exploration of the problem of lynching in America and who had written fictional works on this topic.[13]

Unlike W. E. B. DuBois, who visited China three years later and expressed serious concern regarding Western political and economic domination of the Chinese,[14] Langston Hughes, though appalled by Shanghai vice and discrimination, seemed to enjoy the lighter side of Shanghai life. Black performers, musicians, and dancers had a place in the entertainment world of the treaty ports, and Hughes did not neglect to sample their performances. Possibly DuBois was too elitist to be concerned with this aspect of black life. Chinese writers, however, recognized the importance of the performing arts in black culture and noted this as a characteristic that distinguished black from American culture.[15] But our concern here is with black writers and their works, and both received scant attention in the thirties.

Although twentieth-century Irish works were translated, there were few critical notices regarding them. Yeats's poetry continued to be discussed, as was James Joyce's fiction, which apparently began to be read by Chinese writers. Still, Chinese writers in the thirties, as in the previous decade, were interested in and responsive to foreign literary currents, and they criticized Irish writers for their increasing provincialism. It was stated in 1936 that Irish writers were restricted by their nationalism. Their literary works were confined to particular localities and regions and, therefore, not a single great literary work had appeared in the last few years. Only recently was there a promise that writers like Francis Hacket and Frank O'Connor would break out of this provincialism.[16]

Interest in Yeats was shown by several writers who either commented critically on the poet's work or noted his importance as the leader of the Irish literary renaissance. A brief notice stated that although he was seventy years old, Yeats was ageless and had lost none of his spirit of freedom.[17] Fei Chien-chao emphasized the distinction between the Literary Revival, of which Yeats was not a founder but a participant, and the movement for political independence. To him, the Literary Revival was aimed at having the Irish recognize and protect their national heritage; political independence was something else. Fei believed that, among other reasons, Yeats's importance as a poet was due to his use of language; the language of his poetry was ordinary and simple and resembled prose.[18] Use of language was also the outstanding characteristic of James Joyce's works, wrote Fei, and some said he was a stylist beyond compare. Fei had apparently read Joyce's *Dubliners*, *Ulysses*, and *Portrait of the Artist as a Young Man* and remarked that in these works Joyce emphasized the carnal aspect of human life. In some respect, therefore, he was like Rabelais, although Rabelais also paid attention to the spiritual side which Joyce did not.[19]

Unlike in the twenties, Chinese critics now suggested that outsiders had difficulties understanding present Irish literary trends. Moreover, the great writers of the nineteenth century were no longer popular. "In present-day Ireland," stated one writer, "the average person is no longer fond of Yeats, Synge, and others, who during the fruitful time of the literary movement wrote plays about peasants. . . ." The various brief notices that mentioned contemporary writers like Liam O'Flaherty, Sean O'Casey, or Sean O'Faolain seem to indicate that Chinese writers were not especially moved by their works.[20]

Among Polish writers, Sienkiewicz was mentioned but briefly, although translations of his works continued to appear. More attention was given to Reymont and Żeromski. As in the previous decade, Sienkiewicz was admired for his peasant portrayals, and Reymont's major work, *Peasants*, was apparently well-known also. Żeromski's youthful socialist leanings were mentioned but his works were described as romantic and as using psychological approaches.[21] Janusz Korczak, a Jew, was identified as a Polish writer. Biographical information regarding the well-known educator and writer, who was killed only seven years later together with the two hundred children of his Warsaw Ghetto orphanage, was brief and taken from the Esperanto translation.[22]

The question of language or style was not raised in connection with Polish literature. Possibly the sources that translators consulted for their biographical and critical notes did not make reference to language. The fact that Polish literature was not read in the original does not seem a likely reason. For example, Chao Ching-shen in his discussion of the Jewish writer Moishe Nadir precisely stressed Nadir's simple language, direct speech, and use of idiom, although it is out of the question that Chao read Nadir in the original Yiddish.[23]

The paucity of substantive critical discussions of authors and works is noteworthy. Several reasons may be suggested for this lack. Possibly the foremost reason is the fact that China's literary scene in the thirties was taking new directions. Moreover, Soviet literature came to play an increasingly important role in leftist literary circles. A second consideration may be that fewer works of oppressed peoples were available in China. The fact that Commercial Press, which received the bulk of such works, was bombed out in 1932 cannot be overlooked. The rise of Hitler and its effects on publishing, especially as concerns Harrassowitz in Leipzig—a major source for Esperanto translations of oppressed peoples' literature in China—may also be a factor. And finally, whereas nineteenth-century works of oppressed peoples served Chinese interests in the twenties, they did so to a much lesser degree in the thirties. At the same time, it seems that Chinese writers were unable to discern a clear and general direction in oppressed peoples' literature of the twentieth century.

Translation in the Thirties

The works translated from oppressed peoples' literature in the thirties can be grouped into three overall categories, not substantially different from those in the twenties. The largest category deals with social injustice and its many forms; to the second belong works on political topics; and the third deals with the individual's isolation in society. In the following discussion, representative examples will be summarized, and works of both nineteenth- and twentieth-century authors are included.

Some of the most powerful examples of social injustice came from works of black Americans. There is Claude McKay's battle cry "If We Must Die," [74] which begins: "If we must die let it not be like dogs" and which ends:

> Like men we'll face the murderous, cowardly pack,
> Pressed to the wall, dying, but fighting back!

There is also "Share Croppers", [73] by Langston Hughes, of which the first and last verse read:

> Just a herd of Negroes
> Driven to the field,
> Plowing, planting, hoeing,
> To make the cotton yield.
> . . . .
> Then a herd of Negroes
> Driven to the field
> Plowing life away
> To make the cotton yield.

William Mulder in his "The Uses of Adversity: The Literary Emancipation of the Black American"[24] argues that the hallmarks of black literature coming of age are a new racial attitude and attention to particular black issues, together with a new radicalism. Black writers, nonetheless, also dealt with a universal concern: freedom, even if it was freedom for their own people. Thus, according to Mulder, the universal ingredient was that they said something "about the necessity of freedom itself." Possibly this awareness led to the translation of one chapter of Walter White's *The Fire in the Flint* (1924). [72] White's novel was the first work about blacks who acted like normal human beings and used normal speech rather than dialect. The novel is a powerful statement against lynching, and chapter seventeen, which was translated in 1933, deals with various forms of violence against blacks—rape, killing, and mob brutality.

Injustices perpetrated in times of war, the victims of which are the poor and simple, is the essence of Kaden-Bandrowski's "The Sentence." [85] Jakob, a poor peasant, has remained in a war zone to protect his few pitiful possessions. The Cossacks arrive and give the starving Jakob food. In return he is to show them the way to the village. Jakob is reluctant; he is dimly aware that one ought not to cooperate with the enemy. But the Cossacks beat him brutally and he consents to go. There is a battle; the Cossacks retreat and the Poles return. Jakob is accused of treason. He is bewildered and does not understand the meaning of his crime or why he is to be killed.

For the first time, stories about workers were translated— episodes from the life of the urban proletariat. That small pleasures like outings and recreation are not for them is the message of "The Picnic" [75] by S. Libin, who wrote about American Jewish immigrants at the turn of the century. Libin employs a humorous narrative, but the bitter message is not obscured. A poor capmaker takes his wife and five children on an outing, to breathe fresh air, as he puts it, and to watch how other people enjoy themselves. The venture is a disaster from beginning to end: the children are sick on the crowded train; the lunch does not survive the journey; it rains; the children are hungry. With no money for supper, the capmaker concedes that such pleasures are not for workers.

Several brief stories by the Irish writer Liam O'Flaherty appeared in the mid-thirties. Like his novels, O'Flaherty's short stories expose and condemn social injustice by describing the peasant's back-breaking labor and small rewards. Where Lady Gregory's peasants and poor accepted their lot stoically, patiently,

or even humorously, O'Flaherty's peasants, though often timid, cry
out against it. O'Flaherty has been criticized for minimizing plot
and neglecting literary ornament;[25] and indeed, though his stories
generally explore no more than a specific and circumscribed situa-
tion, the impotence of his peasants' suffering is powerfully conveyed. "A Shilling" [88] is a tale of greed, cunning, and selfish-
ness as well as of the indifference of the rich to the poor, and of
the poor to one another. The plot of the story is simple: one man
accidentally drops a coin and another schemes to obtain it. Told
with utter economy, the author exposes the baseness of human
behavior. Silent protest is the major ingredient in both "Spring
Sowing" [82] and "Poor People" [81]. In the first, a newlywed
couple begins their first spring sowing. Suddenly the bride realizes that from now on she will be chained to cruel poverty and hard
work; chained as a slave to husband and land. She is a peasant's
wife. The feeling of being trapped by poverty, made helpless "by
the great chain of hunger," is expressed still more forcefully in
the second story, where a father waits for his child to die.

The above examples show that, as in the twenties, there was
variety in the works chosen for translation. Similiar to characters
in the stories by Chinese authors of the thirties, wronged peasants
or workers in the translated works, although aware of their
wrongs, do not as yet know how to strike back. One senses, however, that these authors of the poor and the exploited tried to
convey the moment of the turning point. Life had become unbear-
able; whether Irish or Chinese, the peasant should, writers seem
to say, begin to act.

Stories translated on political topics were more varied and
often more sophisticated than in the twenties. They frequently
conveyed a mood of disappointment and futility. One of the best
examples is Żeromski's "The Stronger Sex." [92] Idealism and a
notion to help the poor and stamp out corruption brings a young
physician to a backward village. He soon succumbs to lethargy
and periodic depression. One day he is called to treat a teacher
in a nearby village who has been stricken by typhus. He recognizes her as the girl he had been infatuated with during his student days, and who was referred to as the Darwinist. The girl
dies, and in her possessions the doctor finds a manuscript entitled
"Physics for the People." Remorseful because of his earlier weakness, the doctor resolves to act again. But it does not last and
he soon reverts to his former state of spiritual and intellectual

lassitude. In this story, the Polish author cynically dismisses the populist notions of the intelligentsia—that they are both physically and spiritually suited to peasant life. It also seems that the peasants are not willing to accept populist idealism.

King Macius, The First (1923) by Janusz Korczak is principally a children's book; but like many other children's classics, it imparts messages of social and political value. Korczak's work consists of an exploration and criticism of various political notions: government reforms, political demagoguery and dictatorship, the nature of democracy, war and revolution. Only the first portion of Korczak's book was translated from an Esperanto version by A. Weinstein, [79] and it is therefore quite certain that the Chinese translator was not acquainted with the book in its entirety or intent. In the initial portion translated, Macius, the boy king, demands increasing powers of state for himself, while the old ministers manage and mismanage international affairs. As a result, war is declared almost as an accident and as an act of thoughtless stupidity.[26]

Prus's novella "Outpost" [68] deals with problems of social change in the village, Polish peasant conservatism, and foreign exploitation. The work examines the fate of a peasant family whose lives and relationships with other villagers are radically and painfully changed by three complex events. First of all, the landed aristocracy sells the manor lands, portions of which had been traditionally leased to the peasants. Secondly, a railway is built nearby, transforming the traditional village economy. And finally, the manor land is bought by German colonists who cooperatively and efficiently work the land. Their work methods contrast sharply with the individualistic and inefficient work habits of the Polish peasants. Prus captures with singular sensitivity the land hunger of the Polish peasant as well as his stubborn conservatism. Thoroughly aware of the complex social and economic structures operative in the village, Prus's antiaristocratic and socialist leanings clearly emerge in this work.

Without question, their political and social content provided the impetus for translating Sienkiewicz's "Letters from America." [83] Sienkiewicz's 1876-78 visit to America was financed with a series of letters which were published in Poland. Mao Tun carefully excerpted portions of these letters to make statements on social and political theory. Although the letters are not fictional, their inclusion here further highlights the political nature of a number of translated works in the thirties. Sienkiewicz's subjective descriptions of New York and Chicago led Mao Tun to emphasize (through selective and slanted translations) that even if American democracy did not eliminate social inequities, unlike elsewhere, such inequities did not divide American society into two strata: American respect for labor prevented it. Economic and historical conditions gave rise to this attitude of respect, and social classes never developed. Secondly, the American educational system emphasizes elementary and not higher education. Nowhere else does one find, therefore, as high a degree of political awareness as among the American masses. Thirdly, refinement of manners does not separate the lower from the higher classes as is the case elsewhere, simply because Americans do not attach importance to manners. In sum, concluded Mao Tun, the excellence of American civilization lies in the fact that culture is widely diffused and not the property of a minority, with the majority leading crude, uncultured, and ignorant lives.

A final example in this category is Irish writer Sean O'Faolain's satire "Sullivan's Trousers." [87] As an attack on the New Irish Economic Policy, which attempted to dispense with British imports and insisted on self-sufficiency, the story deals with a specific and timely topic. Its appeal to the Chinese reader may have consisted principally in the colorful and farcical treatment of a complex problem. Financially ruined by the New Economic Policy, Sullivan takes off his trousers, dons kilts, uses flint to light his pipe, and establishes a primitive community of followers. His trouserless life is said to have changed the course of Irish civilization, and a monument is to be erected to Sullivan. Just then Sullivan reappears again in trousers, creating an uproar in the course of which his trousers are pulled off, and Sullivan takes flight. Aside from the hilarious plot, "Sullivan's Trousers" clearly was a means for debunking the notion that a country can turn its back on technological progress and the effects of such progress on everyday life. The revival of the ways of one's forefathers, as a type of conservatism, is not a workable political proposition and surely would not have missed impressing Chinese readers.

Individual isolation in an impersonal society is a major theme in twentieth-century Western literature. Hopeless, the individual despairs and is alienated from the world around him. May Fourth intellectuals had enthusiastically greeted the notion of individual freedom, and "Ibsenism" as championed by Hu Shih and others was much in vogue. So strong was the desire to throw off the shackles of the family—the concomitant of individualism—that the problem of individual loneliness and isolation was hardly even a minor theme in Chinese literature until the latter twenties and thirties. Some stories on this theme were translated in the twenties, but more appeared in the thirties. In "In the Mountains," [80] by the Jewish author H. D. Nomberg, a brooding Jewish student is hopelessly in love with a painter, but his is a world apart from her and her vaguely bohemian surroundings. During a winter excursion to the mountains, in utmost desperation, he kills himself while sledding down a mountainside. Eliza Orzeszkowa's "Do You Remember?" [89] describes the loneliness of the self-made man who left the country for status and affluence in the city. In spite of his prosperity, he is unhappy and dissatisfied, but he does not realize the source of his unhappiness until a letter from his sister arrives. In it, she reminds him of the old village home, the forest, their nursemaid— and he suddenly realizes that in the city he has become rootless.

The play *The God of Vengeance* [84] by Asch develops a number of topics. Although the intent of the play is clearly anti-religious, attempting to expose the hypocrisy and inhumanity of prevalent beliefs, it also deals with the dilemma of the modern Jew who is made rootless by middle-class aspirations for respectability. As such, he is alienated from the traditional, purely religious Jewish community. *The God of Vengeance* is certainly a more complex work than most other translations and possibly testifies to the heightened awareness of crisis that urbanized and bourgeois Shanghai intellectuals themselves faced.[27] The play takes place in a large Polish city where Yankel and his wife run a brothel on the ground floor while their living quarters are in the upper story of the building. They try to protect their daughter both from the prostitutes and from knowledge about their livelihood. Yankel seeks further protection by commissioning the writing of a Torah scroll, a scroll of the law, to be placed in his daughter's bedroom as a talisman against corruption. Such superstitious use of holy writ is condoned by the community leaders because Yankel is expected to give a large contribution for the scroll. However, neither Torah nor the parents' watchfulness helps: a prostitute and her pimp seduce the daughter. The tragedy overwhelms the father but does not touch the community leaders, whose sole concern is with preserving the outward forms of Judaism. They give no thought to the fate of the daughter.

Whereas in the twenties descriptions of oppressed peoples' conditions were related to the works chosen for translation, the emphasis on imperialism in the thirties did not parallel the choice of works to be translated. Similarly, while there was a considerable body of critical and theoretical comments on oppressed peoples' authors and their works in the twenties, such comments in the thirties were few and inconclusive. Chinese translators, writers, and intellectuals in the twenties tried to illuminate their own condition by means of other peoples' literary works, but in the thirties they failed to do so. Indeed, despite explanations of imperialist oppression said to be common to both Chinese and other peoples, the relevance of oppressed peoples' literature to China's condition in the thirties became increasingly difficult to see.

Yet, some Chinese intellectuals continued to reach out to the world, including the particular world of oppressed peoples, even though they no longer clearly explained how this world should be understood. Their attempts to retain some kind of link with the world seem almost desperate when viewed against the threatening cataclysm of the Sino-Japanese War and World War II. It is difficult to say whether such attempts had their root in the cosmopolitanism (misplaced perhaps in the China of the thirties) of some of the leftist writers, or whether the spirit of the twenties, of May Fourth, continued to animate some aspects of the literary and intellectual scene. Whatever the cause, even Chinese Marxists in Yenan, China's hinterland, did not abandon the world until after 1943. The translation of two stories by Peretz [93, 94] for the literary page of *Chieh-fang jih-pao* [Liberation daily] in 1941-42, then under the editorship of Ting Ling, exemplifies this phenomenon.

When, after the establishment of the People's Republic, translation activity was resumed in the fifties, the context of translating was vastly changed. By then, the notion of oppressed peoples and their relationship to China had ceased to be valid and was no longer mentioned. Although some Chinese intellectuals in the fifties again, or perhaps still, reached out to the world, the particular world of oppressed peoples became only briefly relevant, and then in an entirely new sense.

V

TRANSLATING IN THE PEOPLE'S REPUBLIC OF CHINA

Since the establishment of the People's Republic, translating in China has taken place within the political framework and is related to the cultural policy that is current. In the fifties, an unprecedented number of translations from world literature appeared— according to one account, 15,749 works from forty-three countries were translated, and 261 million copies were sold.[1] (This figure does not include shorter pieces which were published in journals.) Translating from foreign literature had a place in cultural and literary life because learning from foreign countries, even if such learning emanated from the bourgeoisie or the feudal classes, was stressed repeatedly by Mao Tse-tung since 1942.[2] Included among translations in the fifties were also works from Polish and Yiddish literature as well as works of black Americans. From Irish literature apparently only one play was translated, and this by the communist author O'Casey. After 1959, translation activities generally fell off, and works from the socialist countries of Eastern Europe ceased to appear around 1962. According to Galik, the Sino-Soviet conflict is to be held responsible for this.[3]

Translation activities ceased altogether by 1966, the year that marked the beginning of the Great Proletarian Cultural Revolution. Although translating was resumed around 1973 or 1974, apparently nothing was published until after Mao's death in September 1976 and following the purge of the so-called "Gang of Four" in October of that year. The "Gang of Four" has been accused of strangulating Chinese literary and artistic life. Following their removal from the political scene, a new cultural policy was announced under the 1957 slogan "Let a hundred flowers bloom, let a hundred schools contend." To this was added one further slogan, "Make the past serve the present and foreign things serve China" *(Ku wei chin yung, yang wei chung yung)*. The latter, as part of the new cultural policy, allows once more for the resumption of translation activities.[4]

Lu Hsün's authority for the importance of translating was invoked already in October 1976. About half of Lu Hsün's works, it was stated, were translations and introductions to foreign literature. He acquainted Chinese readers with more than one hundred foreign authors, and he emphasized the literature of oppressed peoples. To Lu Hsün, the work of translation was an integral part of the revolutionary cause.[5] Since the autumn of 1976, translation work has apparently progressed apace, with such authors as Turgenev, Gorky, Mark Twain, Chekhov, and even Ibsen appearing again in Chinese. Authors of the smaller European countries are represented in at least one collection of short stories. The principle governing the selection of works for translation since 1976 is that such works must reflect important social problems of the time and that they must skillfully portray the thought content.[6] In other words, the contents must lend themselves to presently acceptable political interpretations.

Both nineteenth- and twentieth-century works were chosen for translation in the fifties. From contemporary Polish literature, works dealing with World War II, the Polish Resistance, and post-war reconstruction were selected. Aside from full-length novels which were published as separate editions, translations of poetry, drama, and short stories appeared in the journal *Translations* edited by Mao Tun. Its successor, as of January 1959, was *Shih-chieh wen-hsüeh* [World literature]. It was edited by Ts'ao Ching-hua and featured occasional translations. Neither journal described the state or fate of the peoples whose literary works appeared in its pages, and there were few critical articles about authors and works. In addition to English and Esperanto sources, Russian as well as German translations were used, and a few translators apparently worked directly from Polish.

Comments on Authors and their Works

Turning first to critical comments on Polish literature, it is noteworthy that Chinese writers tended to translate essays by Polish critics rather than write evaluations themselves. Should this be taken to mean that Chinese writers or translators had nothing to say about Polish authors and their works? Not necessarily. Instead, it may indicate an uncertainty of how to evaluate nineteenth- or early twentieth-century works within the context of revolutionary literature. The fifties required that even the writings of the bourgeoisie have redeeming features. Writers were possibly playing it safe when they left it up to Polish critics to ferret out such features. Nevertheless, in some cases translators appended notes to the translation, clearly attempting to justify the translation in accordance with Marxist theory.

Among essays translated from Polish, a lengthy article concerning the nineteenth-century poet-patriot Adam Mickiewicz is of some interest. Essentially a biobibliographical summary, it stresses the revolutionary nature of Mickiewicz's works, his sympathy for oppressed peoples as well as his political importance and wide influence on others who were not Polish.[7]

A note appended to the translated stories by Reymont highlights the political aspects of the writer and his works. The biographical details of the writer's life focus predictably on Reymont's working class experience and peasant background. Still, although Reymont recognized the dual contradictions between peasants and landed gentry and rich and poor peasants, wrote the translator, he was handicapped in resolving them. In his works he adopted the viewpoint of a member of the propertied class. Although Reymont recognized the ills of a rapidly developing capitalism at the end of the nineteenth century, he did not understand the historical process of social development. At the same time, Reymont's real worth was distorted by Polish critics who regarded him as a naturalistic writer, when in fact he was the greatest genius of realistic art in Poland.[8]

Sean O'Casey was not a problem for the Chinese critic. As a communist, the Irish writer and dramatist, whose play *The Star Turns Red* appeared in *Translations,* was praised without reservations by Wang Tso-liang. O'Casey's works were excellent, wrote Wang, because he was a communist. Wang was apparently acquainted with O'Casey's plays and commented on most of them, noting that they dealt with social and political struggles in their many forms. Like writers of the thirties who rarely failed to note the use of language by Irish writers, Wang, too, emphasized the manner in which O'Casey handled the language of urban workers.[9]

Among Yiddish writers, Shalom Aleichem received considerable attention and warm praise. On the occasion of the centennial of his birth, a commemorative meeting was held in Peking at which Mao Tun, one of his major translators, paid tribute to the great author and gave a reading from his works. It was announced at the meeting that two translations, *Mottel, The Cantor's Son*, and *Menahem Mendl*, were to appear shortly.[10] Elsewhere, Shalom Aleichem was described as a writer who came from the people and who wrote about small places and small people, of oppression and the oppressed. By means of humor and a humorous style, he exposed the ugly aspects of capitalism. In fact, among his more than three hundred short stories, the most important were those that described Jewish life under Czarist despotism and capitalist oppression. His works may be considered a valuable contribution to the treasury of world literature.[11] The translator of Shalom Aleichem's *The Great Fair* appended a brief note to the book. Shalom Aleichem, he stated, wrote carefully about the Jewish people's *(jen-min)* customs. He used colorful descriptions when writing about the past and Jewish religion.[12] A brief comment on the "Song of Songs" stories is especially noteworthy. These stories, wrote the editor, helped young people form new ideals. They expressed a pitiless rebellion against the family and rejected traditional customs. The stories showed that the spirit of the new times has already begun to be part of the thoughts of young people.[13] Lastly, a brief biographical comment on Y. L. Peretz stressed that the author had participated in illegal activities of organizing workers, that he opposed oppression, and that in some of his works he described the rising strength of the Jewish workers' movement.[14]

The problem of black Americans has been especially noted in the People's Republic. In 1963 Mao Tse-tung issued a statement on behalf of America's blacks, calling attention to the "sharpening of class struggle and national struggle" in America.[15] But critical comments regarding their literary works have been scarce. Even the 1963 *World Literature* issue, which was dedicated to black literature, contained only two articles by Chinese authors, and these were not on literary topics. One, by the noted woman writer Ping Hsing, was a tribute to W. E. B. DuBois; the other dealt with the black NAACP leader, Robert William, who fled to Cuba.[16] In 1959 W. E. B. DuBois and his wife, Shirley Graham, visited China. Whereas DuBois's visit in 1936 had been barely mentioned in the press, in 1959 he was an honored guest of the state. During his two-month stay, DuBois and his wife traveled throughout China; he was given a gala ninety-first birthday party and he lectured on the rebirth of Africa. The Chinese press hailed him as the Father of African independence. Kuo Mo-jo's poem for the occasion refers to "our colored peoples" and the glory that DuBois adds to them.[17]

While in Peking, both DuBois and Shirley Graham lectured on black literature. Shirley Graham's lecture "Blacks in American Literature" was translated into Chinese and published in *Translations*.[18] For Chinese writers who listened to and read her lecture, she no doubt provided an excellent overview on black writers. According to the Chinese translation, Graham's critical criteria were, however, not always political but were more concerned with a black writer's relationship to white America. Thus, of Langston Hughes, for example, she said that he gave up the struggle after World War II and settled for writing works ingratiating to white America.

Not much of significance was stated in these sparse comments. And yet, the fact that they were made at all requires some sort of explanation; for, aside from O'Casey, a twentieth-century communist writer, what possible relationship would Chinese writers in the fifties find with nineteenth-century Polish or Yiddish writers? An answer is suggested by Levenson's distinction of *min-tsu* and *jen-min*. Both terms are used for peoples, but both have different meanings. *Min-tsu,* as peoples, signifies an organic national entity. It was the term used in the twenties and thirties for oppressed peoples. *Jen-min,* as used in the People's Republic, stands for peoples in class relationships. Peoples anywhere are *jen-min,* and all *jen-min* have a common cause.[19] Shalom Aleichem is referred to as a *jen-min* writer, a people's writer, and not a *min-tsu* or a national people's writer. The change in terminology implies that peoples everywhere, including the Chinese, are joined in a common goal. This goal is no longer one of national definition or assertion, but it is an international goal directed against imperialism, class (not national) oppression and exploitation. *Jen-min* as peoples thus suggested an entirely different relationship of Chinese to others; it implied relationships within an international brotherhood. There is here a slight resemblance to the universalism discussed earlier, but internationalism in a political sense is not universalism in a cultural sense.

Another reason that Chinese writers and translators in the fifties took note of nineteenth-century Polish and Yiddish writers may be because the works of both were said to express the spirit of humanism. Chinese writers in the fifties frequently justified their continuing appreciation for the great works of European realism by pointing to their humanist qualities. Shalom Aleichem as well as Reymont were referred to as humanist writers (*jen-tao*

chu-i che).[20] The issue of humanism, however, was a thorny one
for orthodox Marxist critics because of the bourgeois implications
and the supraclass associations that could be deduced from it.
Humanism might also imply "common human nature," or "things common to all people"; humanism was suspect. Indicative of this sus-
picion are the charges brought by the Party against writers and
critics at the end of the fifties and the beginning of the sixties.[21]
That translations of nineteenth-century Polish and Yiddish writers
ceased shortly thereafter may very well be related to the problem
inherent in the question of humanism and Marxist literary theory.

Works Translated

Although nineteenth- and twentieth-century authors were
translated in the fifties and a fairly wide range of themes was
selected, these translations do not readily allow for categorization,
as did their predecessors in the twenties and thirties. From Irish
literature there is only Sean O'Casey's play *The Star Turns Red*.
From Yiddish literature there are stories by nineteenth-century
authors, Shalom Aleichem and Y. L. Peretz, but no twentieth-
century works. From black literature there is a quantity of
twentieth-century poetry and several stirring nineteenth-century
calls for resistance to slavery. From Polish literature alone there
is a fairly wide sampling of authors and themes, due perhaps to
the personal contacts that Chinese and Polish authors maintained
during the fifties through mutual visits and writers' conferences.
Thus, in the absence of categories, the following discussion will
diverge from the pattern maintained in previous chapters and will
show instead the kinds of works translated from each literature.

Two general characteristics can be noted among Polish works
chosen for translation. Those from the nineteenth century usually
have a rebellious if not revolutionary kernel, aside from what may
be termed their humanistic content. The strength of the human
spirit in adversity is shown at its best. Those from the twentieth
century generally deal with social or political resistance to oppression, establishment of the new order, and, especially, the heroic
resistance against German aggression in World War II.

From the nineteenth century, there is "The Returning Wave."
[100] The story deals with a German factory owner who exploits
Polish workers while his son squanders money abroad and at home.

Disaster overtakes both family and factory when the son dies of a
dueling wound and a machinist dies of injuries sustained at work.
The story is a strong condemnation of foreign exploitation and
labor abuse.

Similar to "The Outpost," published in 1930, "Michael" [98]
also shows the influence of the railroad on peasant life. When
trains began to reach villages, peasants had new alternatives to
rural poverty. Michael is a homeless orphan, with no future in
the village. He decides to go to Warsaw to try his luck. There
the peasant boy finds work carrying bricks on construction sites.
But he is lonely and lost—a wretchedly poor peasant boy in a
foreign city with its incomprehensible ways—exploited as a worker
and abused as a simpleton. Prus's sensitive portrayal of Michael,
the poor peasant lad who ever so tentatively reaches out toward
more than mere village subsistence, is matched by his portrayal
of "Antek." [160] Antek is different. He is a dreamer who carves
windmills, houses, and crosses from wood. For a boy such as
Antek, with stars in his eyes, there is no place in the village. He
leaves for the city in search of learning and in pursuit of his
dreams.

Prus, the author of these stories, has deep sympathy for his
heroes, who are the young and with whom lies the future. At the
same time, he unequivocally condemns economic parasites and the
rich. His young people are resilient and honest—they will survive
and overcome because their spirit is strong and they have the
courage to enter a world that is changing. Neither Michael nor
Antek are victims in spite of abject poverty and the great difficulties before them.

Eliza Orzeszkowa's "Years of Draught" [139] also condemns
exploitation, but she makes an even stronger statement on behalf
of the oppressed. Where Prus's world included the countryside as
well as the city, the peasant condition was the central problem in
all of Orzeszkowa's works.[22] "Years of Draught" deals with the
Polish famine of 1854-56. Orzeszkowa skillfully contrasts the life of
the landed gentry with that of a peasant family. The peasants are
starving. Young and old die as the great hunger spreads. But
the rich, oblivious to the peasants' suffering, continue their
amusements and pleasures.

Anti-Americanism may have motivated the translation of two stories by Sienkiewicz. Like the stories translated in the thirties, these, too, were based on his American journey. "Orso" [103] criticizes American attitudes toward and treatment of Indians, while "For Bread" [104] depicts the bitter and often hopeless fate of Polish immigrants in America.

Turning to twentieth-century Polish authors and their works, we find very different themes, and the choice of works translated seems far more random.23 "Jozefòw," [102] by Adolf Rudnicki, is the name of a summer resort outside of Warsaw. There, in the winter of 1936, congregate a group of people, among them a young Jewish radical who is dying of consumption. His last words are uttered in praise of the fighting Spanish proletariat, and he, as their Polish comrade, sends his greetings to Spain. Undoubtedly, Chinese readers of the fifties could readily identify with radicalized, though bourgeois intellectuals. These were familiar to them from Chinese works of twenty-odd years ago. In addition, there is in this story the emphasis on internationalism and the common battle against fascism.

"Village Wedding," [121] by Maria Dąbrowska, deals with the present. The specific problem of the story is whether the peasants should join the agricultural cooperative. Dąbrowska left no doubt that Polish peasants did not unanimously support the formation of rural cooperatives. In Chinese stories of the fifties, this was not an unfamiliar problem. There were peasants who wanted to join, and there were peasants who were against joining because they did well on their own. However, where the Chinese author usually ended his story on a positive note, Dąbrowska's ending was inconclusive. In postwar socialist Poland, Dąbrowska continued to be a realistic writer who did not resort to socialist realism.

A number of works about war-stricken Poland were translated into Chinese. Among these, Wanda Wasilewska's *Rainbow*,24 which was first published in 1944, is a novel in the heroic-partisan-peasant-resistance tradition, replete with incompetent Germans and victorious Red Army soldiers. Plot and stock characters are all too familiar from much of anti-Japanese resistance literature, and even the Ukrainian landscape is easily transposed to Manchuria or North China.

"Holy Week,"[25] by Jerzy Andrzejewski, was also written
during World War II. One wonders to what extent Chinese readers
could integrate the content of this story with their own war experiences. The story deals with the Warsaw Ghetto uprising in 1943,
but as experienced by an upper-class assimilated Jewish woman who
is outside the ghetto. Shunned by her former Polish friends, she
is refused shelter and protection; certain death awaits her. The
author expresses both horror and revulsion—horror at what tran-
spired in the Warsaw Ghetto, and revulsion against Polish anti-
Semitism and the population's indifference to the Jewish tragedy.

Twentieth-century authors like Dąbrowska and Wasilewska
dealt with topics that were familiar to most readers in socialist
countries. In these works, the authors tended to understate particular or individual responses to universal problems and tragic
situations were of a different dimension. The same is true for
Sean O'Casey's play *The Star Turns Red*. [138] The setting may
be Dublin in 1913, but the problem concerns the fighting proletariat led by incorruptible communists against capitalist exploiters,
corrupt bourgeoisie, and brutal fascists. The wavering masses
and the divided church each have a part in the play. And there
is the inevitable final battle and equally inevitable proletarian victory. As in Chinese fiction of the fifties, villains and heroes are
clearly recognizable, as are, indeed, wavering peasants.

From nineteenth-century Yiddish literature, there are
Shalom Aleichem's sensitive stories about children who daydream
of a better world and the poor who try to manage in an increasingly
complex world. "A Page from the 'Song of Songs'," "Another Page
from the 'Song of Songs'," and "Final Pages from the 'Song of
Songs'" [157] (the three stories are translated under one title) is
a story of love that begins in childhood but cannot mature because
imperceptibly Jewish life has begun to change. Traditions are
broken. The young man, who once would have followed the ways
of the father, now has the option of leaving the village. He can
obtain a secular education "outside." The girl still remains at
home. Sorrowfully she recognizes her backwardness and the inequality that has developed between her and the young man in
adulthood. The Chinese editor describes this story as one that
depicts pitiless rebellion against the family and a rejection of traditional customs.[26] Perhaps; but Shalom Aleichem also conveyed
in this story the pain inflicted and the hurt received at the moment
of change. It is a moment of irretrievable loss.

"Bad Luck" [150] similarly deals with the world of growing alternatives, but here the treatment is humorous. The story is the last of a series concerning the exploits of Menahem Mendl, a man who will try his hand at any business. His adventures are told in the form of letters to his wife at home. The last episode, as translated into Chinese, finds Menahem Mendl in Bessarabia, incongruously trying to sell life insurance. Predictably, he fails and must flee for his life. But now he escapes for good— to America, where he expects to become rich at last.

Part of Shalom Aleichem's greatness is his uncanny ability to capture Jewish society as changes imperceptibly intruded. The old ways still remained, but new ways began, and a particular lifestyle with its very own rhythm and values began to disappear forever. If the author permitted himself moments of nostalgia, he, however, also professed courageous optimism. Possibly, it was this quality of optimism that induced Chinese translators to translate Shalom Aleichem's stories.

The stories by Y. L. Peretz that were chosen for translation have a different spirit. Among these, "A Weaver's Love" [140] is especially interesting. In this story, the author lashed out at social injustice and, furthermore, considered change in negative terms. The story is told through letters that the weaver writes to a shoemaker whose sister he wants to marry. The weaver describes the exploitation of labor in textile plants and the inability of workers to organize in order to protect themselves. Peretz especially attacked the notion of the new freedom. To be sure, the individual worker is free to work or not work, but unfortunately, he depends on the manufacturer and not the other way around. Bitterly, Peretz's weaver comments that they are weaving linens and woolens as well as shrouds for the "good and pious world that we once knew." In its place will be a new and rotten world.

Translations from nineteenth- and twentieth-century black literature were nearly all poems. Revolutionary fervor, rejection of oppression, blacks asserting themselves in the white man's world— these are the motifs not only in the pre-selected anthology *Hei-jen shih-hsüan* [Selections from black poetry][27] but also in the 1963 *World Literature* issue dedicated to black literature. Represented are such well-known poets as Frances E. W. Harper, Claude McKay, Langston Hughes, Robert E. Hayden, and Margaret Walker. Their voices, strong and assured, weave black history, written in

blood, into a present that holds out the promise of a better future.
The poems detail the specifically black experience, but this experience sounds neither strange nor peculiar in Chinese translation.
The poems have an obvious appeal to anyone who has felt the power
of oppression and the yearning for justice and freedom. Here are
the first lines of Hayden's "Gabriel": [126]

> Black Gabriel, riding
> To the gallows tree,
> In this last hour
> What do you see?
>
> "I see a thousand
> thousand slaves
> Rising up
> From forgotten graves,
> . . . ."

The same sentiment is expressed in the final lines of Margaret
Walker's "For My People": [147]

> Let a new earth arise. Let another world be born.
> Let a bloody peace be written . . . let the dirges
> disappear. Let a race of men now rise and take
> control.

Among prose works, several mid-nineteenth-century brief
pieces are impressive for their eloquence. Two examples are
Frederick Douglass's "Men of Color to Arms," [162] a call to enlist
after emancipation, and "A Public Call for Rebellion" [164] by
H. H. Garnet. These pieces had been selected from Herbert
Aptheker's anthology, And Why Not Every Man? (1961), a book
that contains a large variety of documentary materials, many with
stronger revolutionary content than those translated.[28]

Some of the works translated in the fifties and early sixties may have been individually chosen, but the majority were
not. Translating was a part of literary policy, and whether or
not a translation would be published was decided by the literary
establishment, that is, the various literary organs through which
control was maintained over literary and artistic activities.
Much of what was translated and published was of dubious quality, although one must keep in mind that all information on
translating and publishing is fragmentary. Other works

may have appeared in provincial journals, but they are not available to bibliographers or to readers outside China.

Perhaps the humanistic content of nineteenth-century Yiddish and Polish works held some interest, or perhaps the black unrest in America was considered to have wider significance—but in spite of the continued translating of oppressed peoples' literature, it was certainly not seen as the many-faceted phenomenon it had been in the twenties or even thirties. The near absence of critical comments and discussions is significant, as is the fact that earlier translators, like Mao Tun, no longer translated after 1949.

On the whole, the works that were translated met the criteria of what was considered to be revolutionary literature. If the focus of a piece was the evils of the old society, there was generally also the more or less explicitly stated hope for change. Works were chosen with a view toward showing characters who were no longer passive victims but who actively sought by some means to improve their condition. The starkly negative works by Pinski were not translated, perhaps because they were not available, but more likely because Pinski's naturalistic portrayals made them unacceptable. The fact that earlier works, in addition to those of socialist realism, continued to engage the literary bureaucracy (which controlled translation activity) reflects Chinese literary interests in the fifties and early sixties. In spite of cultural and literary policies which imposed limitations on writers' creativity, a number of novels and stories they wrote prior to the Cultural Revolution show that socialist realism and political dictates could be successfully and acceptably circumvented.[29] That translations of oppressed peoples' literature ceased to be published shows, therefore, not the absence of interest but the degree to which controls were imposed over the literary field.

A SUMMARY

The large framework selected in this study for what is, after all, a minor theme was not unintentional. The translating of literary works is a unique activity relevant to both intellectual and literary history. Oppressed peoples and their literature, presented here as a case study, will, it is hoped, stimulate investigations of other literatures in Chinese translation. Investigations of this nature demand a larger framework if we are to grasp some of the subtler trends that are part of the many and often contradictory currents in modern Chinese intellectual and literary history.

The major portion of this study is concerned with May Fourth and its antecedents. New Culture, the meaning of renaissance, and the Literary Revolution together with the importance of language reform are emphasized. The reason is obvious: it was in the twenties that large-scale translation activity was initiated, but the roots of the interest in other people's literature are found in the early years of the twentieth century. The post-May Fourth period, however, is also important. When the thirties are viewed through the prism of oppressed peoples and their literature, one is impressed by the degree to which political issues dominated literary considerations, and how rapidly some major precepts of May Fourth ceased to be heard.

In the fifties, although the earlier assumption that Western literature is important to Chinese cultural life was reiterated, there was in fact no clear statement on why oppressed peoples' literature continued to be translated. Just as the bold critical comments on oppressed peoples' literature in the twenties tell us much about the spirit and temper of May Fourth, the near absence of comments in the fifties may very well indicate the confusion and struggle that characterized the Chinese literary world after Liberation. In the twenties, oppressed peoples' literature was translated for purposefully defined reasons; the people themselves, as well as the authors of this literature, were considered by some to have a specific relevance to China's condition. In the fifties, oppressed peoples' literature was translated for less obvious reasons. The use of a specific terminology *(min-tsu* versus *jen-min)* provides a clue in regard to relevance.

There is, however, one far more important factor in the contrast between the fifties and the decades of the twenties and thirties. As long as China was considered weak, exploited, and humiliated, oppressed peoples could be viewed as beacons of light and their literature exemplary as a tool for changing the condition in China. But the revolutionaries, prior to and after 1949, rejected the image of a weak China. That oppression existed could be acknowledged, but China had gone from weakness to strength, from oppression to independence. Oppression as a historical issue might be curious, undoubtedly interesting, but it did not arouse passion.

Motives for translating thus varied in accordance with changing conditions, ideology, and changing attitudes. And since this study has been concerned with why people translate, we must finally also ask why translating has resumed after 1976, and why it is presently underscored as an important activity. There is no ready answer and cultural policy in the People's Republic is rarely predictable. Several points, nonetheless, deserve to be noted. Articles that stress the importance of translating Russian, English, French, and German works also emphasize that works of Third World writers should be translated.[1] Who, from the official literary point of view, are Third World writers? And will at least a portion of China's Third World consist of oppressed peoples?

The second point is that much of the work produced (or not produced) twenty-odd years ago is now being criticized. According to one writer, translations in the fifties were prepared indiscriminately, works of poor quality were chosen, and there was much duplication. Critical works were few and they were often immature, if not erroneous.[2] All this is to be remedied now. The present call to resume translating, therefore, is not a simple return to the policies of the fifties. Nor is China in the seventies the same as in the fifties; shifts in ideology are obvious. Thus, it is a curious fact that the resumption of translation activity coincides with a changing political climate in post-Maoist China. After a long period of insulation and isolation, the Chinese are reestablishing political, commercial, and intellectual links with the world outside. One of these links is significantly the translating and publishing of works of Western fiction, including works of oppressed peoples.[3]

ABBREVIATIONS

CPFC	*Ch'en-pao fu-chien* [Morning paper supplement].
CPFK	*Ch'en-pao fu-k'an* [Morning post supplement].
FNPL	*Fu-nü p'ing-lun* [Women's critic].
HCH	*Hsin chung-hua* [New China].
HCN	*Hsin ching-nien* [New youth].
HJ	*Hsüeh-jen* [Snowmen], by Shen Yen-ping. Shanghai: Kaiming, 1929.
HJSH	*Hei-jen shih-hsüan* [Selections from black poetry], by Chang Ch'i. Peking: Tso-chia ch'u pan-she, 1957.
HKWCHSC	*Hsien-k'o-wei-chih hsiao-shuo chi* [Collection of short stories by Sienkiewicz], trans. Wang Lu-yen. Shanghai: Kaiming, n.d. (1920s).
HSLHJC	*Hu Shih liu-hsüeh jih-chi* [Hu Shih's student diary]. 4 vols. Taipei, Taiwan: Commercial Press, 1959. Reprint ed.
HSWT	*Hu Shih wen-ts'un* [Hu Shih's collected works]. 4 vols. Taipei, Taiwan: Yüan-t'ung, 1953.
HSYP	*Hsiao-shuo yüeh-pao* [Short story monthly].
HT	*Hsien-tai* [Les contemporains].
HTHSIT	*Hsien-tai hsiao-shuo i-ts'ung* [Translation collection of contemporary fiction], trans. Chou Tso-jen. Shanghai: Commercial Press, 1932. First published in 1922.
HTTMC	*Hsien-tai tu-mu chu* [Contemporary one-act plays]. Tung-fang wen-k'u series, vol. 82. Shanghai: Commercial Press, 1924.

94

HYTHSC	*Hsin yu-t'ai hsiao-shuo chi* [Collection of Yiddish fiction], trans. Shen Yen-ping and Shen Tse-min. Shanghai: Commercial Press, 1924.
ICHHICK	*I-ch'ang huan-hsi i-ch'ang k'ung* [Poor and happy], Hsiao-lo-mu, Ah-lai-han-mu [Shalom Aleichem]. Peking: Jen-min wen-hsüeh, 1959.
IW	*I-wen* [Translations].
KTK	*K'ung ta ku* [Drums], trans. Chou Tso-jen. Originally published as *Tien-ti* [Drops]. Shanghai: Kaiming, 1928.
OCTLHSC	*Ou-chou ta-lu hsiao-shuo chi* [Modern continental short stories]. Tung-fang wen-k'u series, vol. 78. Shanghai: Commercial Press, 1932.
PLTPHSC	*Po-lan t'uan-p'ien hsiao-shuo chi* [A collection of Polish short stories], trans. Shih Chih-ts'un. 2 vols. Wang Yün-wu, ed., Wan-yu wen-k'u series, no. 434. Changsha: Commercial Press, 1939. First published in 1936.
PLWHIL	*Po-lan wen-hsüeh i-luan* [A slice of Polish literature]. 2 vols. Shanghai: Commercial Press, n.d. (1920s).
PSCC	*Pin-ssu-ch'i chi* [Pinski collection], ed. Wang Lu-yen. Shanghai: Commercial Press, n.d. (1920s).
SCWH	*Shih-chieh wen-hsüeh* [World literature].
TFTC	*Tung-fang tsa-chih* [Eastern miscellany].
TT	*Tien-ti* [Drops], trans. Chou Tso-jen. Later republished as *K'ung ta ku* [Drums]. 2 vols. Shanghai: Ya-tung, 1920.
WH	*Wen-hsüeh* [Literature].
WHCP	*Wen-hsüeh chou-pao* [Literature weekly].

WIYK   *Wen-i yüeh-k'an* [Literary art monthly].

WKKP   *Wan-kuo kung-pao* [The globe magazine].

YHCKTHCC *Yo-han Ching-ku ti hsi-ch'u chi* [Collection of John Synge's plays], trans. Kuo Mo-jo. Shanghai: Commercial Press, 1926.

YTHSC   *Yu-t'ai hsiao-shuo chi* [Collection of Jewish fiction], trans. Lu-yen. Shanghai: Kaiming, n.d. (1920s).

YWHSC   *Yü-wai hsiao-shuo chi* [Collection of foreign short stories], trans. Chou Tso-jen. Shanghai: Ch'ün-i shu-she, 1920. First published in Japan in 1909.

NOTES

Introduction

1. Hans J. Störig, *Das Problem Des Übersetzens* (Stuttgart: Henry Govents Verlag, 1963), p. x.

2. Renato Poggioli, "The Added Artificer," in *On Translation*, ed. Reuben A. Brower (New York: Oxford University Press, 1966), p. 147.

3. Joseph T. Shaw, "Literary Indebtedness and Comparative Literary Studies," in *Comparative Literature, Method and Perspective*, ed. Newton P. Stallknecht and Horst Frenz (Carbondale: Southern Illinois University Press, 1961), p. 66.

4. Leo Lowenthal, "The Reception of Dostoevsky's Works in Germany, 1880-1920," in *The Arts in Society*, ed. Robert N. Wilson (Englewood Cliffs, New Jersey: Prentice Hall, 1964), pp. 122-47.

5. Jaroslav Prusek, "A Confrontation of Traditional Oriental Literature with Modern European Literature in the Context of the Chinese Literary Revolution," *Archiv Orientalni* 32, no. 3 (1964): 373.

6. Ibid., p. 371.

7. See J. Prusek, "Studies in Modern Chinese Literature," *Schriften der Sektion für Sinologie bei der Deutschen Akademie der Wissenschaften zu Berlin*, Ostasiatische Forschungen, Heft 2 (Berlin: Akademie Verlag GMBH, 1964), p. 38; and Howard C. Boorman, "Literature and Politics in Contemporary China," Institute of Asian Studies, St. John's University, reprint no. 2, pp. 102-7.

8. See Diana T. Laurenson and Alan Swingewood, *The Sociology of Literature* (New York: Schocken Books, 1972).

9. "Conference of Translators," *Chinese Literature* 1 (1955): 193-94; "Introducing *'I-wen'*—World Literature," *Chinese Literature* 2 (1955): 165-68; and Huang Chia-te, *Fan-i lun-chi* [Selected essays on translation] (Shanghai: Hsi-fang she, 1940), p. 7.

10. For example, Liang Ch'i-ch'ao, "Fan-i yü tao-te hsin-chih kuan-hsi" [The relationship of translating and moral sense], *Hsin-min ts'ung-pao* [The new citizen] 25 (1902): 73-75.

11. "Chen-i, shun-i, wai-i" [Faithful translation, smooth translation, distorted translation], *WH* 2, no. 3 (March 1933): 366-67. See also Wu Shu-t'ien, ed., *Fan-i lun* [Concerning translation] (Shanghai: Kuang-hua, 1933).

12. Yeh Kung-ch'ao, "Lun fan-i yü wen-tzu-ti kai-tsao" [On translating and reconstruction of the written language], *Hsin-yüeh* [Crescent moon] 4 (March 1933): 1-2.

13. "'Fan-i' ho 'p'i-p'ing' fan-i" ["Interpretative" and "critical" translation], *WH* 4, no. 3 (March 1935): 413-15; and Ch'ang Nai-wei, "I-wen-ti feng-ko" [The style of translation], *Wen-hsüeh tsa-chih* [Literary review] 3, no. 4 (1948): 23-26.

14. Huang Chia-te, *Fan-i lun-chi,* pp. 110-16; and Hu Feng, *Wen-i pi-t'an* [Literary discussions] (Shanghai: Sheng-huo, 1937), pp. 325-26.

Chapter I Notes

1. A useful summary is found in Mary C. Wright's "Introduction: The Rising Tide of Change," in *China in Revolution: The First Phase, 1900-1913,* ed. Mary C. Wright (New Haven and London: Yale University Press, 1968), pp. 1-63.

2. Lin Yutang, *A History of the Press and Public Opinion in China* (Shanghai: Kelley and Walsh, 1936), p. 88. See also Tsung Hyui-puh, "Chinese Translations of Western Literature," *Chinese Social and Political Science Review* 12, no. 3 (1928): 396, who stresses the profit motive.

3. Hu Shih, "Shih-ch'i nien-ti hui-ku" [Looking back at seventeen years], in *HSWT* (1924 ed.), vol. 2, chüan 3, pp. 1-5.

4. For an excellent discussion on the women's press, see Charlotte L. Beahan, "Feminism and Nationalism in the Chinese Women's Press, 1902-1911," *Modern China* 1, no. 4 (October 1975): 379-416.

5. "Ko-sheng chiao-yü hui-chih" [Report on education from the provinces], *TFTC* 2, no. 11 (December 1905): 287.

6. Huang Tsun-hsien, *Jen-ching lu shih tsao* [Poems from the hut of human habitation], anno. Ch'ien Chung-lien (Taipei: Chung-hua shu-chü, 1961), pp. 19-20.

7. These and subsequent materials on Poland are based in part on my earlier article "Poland and Polish Authors in Modern Chinese Literature and Translation," *Monumenta Serica* 31 (1974-75): 407-45.

8. Liang Ch'i-ch'ao, "Po-lan mieh-wang chi" [Record of the destruction of Poland], in his *Yin-ping shih chuan-chi* [Collection of essays and addresses] (Shanghai: Chung-hua, 1941), 4:1-3. The essay was originally published in 1896. Liang obtained his information from Hsü Ching-lo's translation of Walter K. Kelly's *The History of Russia from the Earliest Period to the Present Time,* 2 vols. (London: H. G. Bohn, 1854-55). Hsü's translation had been available from the 1890s, if not earlier. See his "O-shih chi-i" [Collected translations on Russian history], 4 chüan, in *Hsi-hsüeh fu-ch'iang ts'ung-shu* [Compendium on wealth and power in Western studies], comp. Chang Yin-huan (Hung-wen-shu chü-shih yin-pen, 1896), ts'e 18-19.

9. K'ang Yu-wei, "Po-lan fen mieh-chi" [Record of the partition and fall of Poland]. The memorial is no longer in existence. For K'ang's reference to it, see Lo Jung-pang, *K'ang Yu-wei, A Biography and Symposium* (Tucson: University of Arizona Press, 1967), p. 105. K'ang probably obtained his information from Liang's article.

10. "Chung-kuo yü Po-lan chih pi-chiao" [China and Poland compared], *TFTC* 1, no. 8 (August 1904): 163-64.

11. "Yu-t'ai jen chih hsien-chuang" [Unrest among the Jews], *WKKP* 17, no. 8 (August 1905): 24-25. For background of the stormy controversy, see Robert G. Weisbord, *African Zion, The Attempt to Establish a Jewish Colony in the East African Protectorate* (Philadelphia: The Jewish Publication Society of America, 1968).

12. Liang Ch'i-ch'ao, "Hsin ta-lu yu-chi" [A record of travels in the new world], in his *Yin-ping shih chuan-chi* (Shanghai: Chung-hua, 1941), 5:1-147. The essay was originally published in 1904.

13. Liang Ch'i-ch'ao, "Mei-kuo ta-t'ung ling pa yung Hei-jen" [America's high command seeks to use blacks], *Hsin-min ts'ung-pao* 29 (14 March 1903): 74-75.

14. Tung wu-fan i-shu (original author?), "Mei-kuo Hei-jen chih chin-chuang" [Present affairs of American blacks], trans. Chi Li-fei, *WKKP* 18, no. 6 (July 1906): 13-17.

15. *WKKP* 17, no. 197 (May 1905): 31.

16. See *Min-li pao* [The democrat], no. 338, p. 2233; no. 344, p. 2275; no. 347, p. 2296, all September 1911.

17. *Records of the Triennial Meeting of the Educational Association of China,* (meeting held in Shanghai on 24 May 1893) (Shanghai: The American Presbyterian Press, 1893), pp. 14-15, 17, 55-62.

18. *Records, China Centenary Missionary Conference,* (conference held in Shanghai, 25 April to 8 May 1907) (Shanghai: Centenary Conference Committee, 1907), pp. 207-8. Perhaps DeFrancis's criticism that the missionaries perpetuated the north-south cleavage by this dual approach of dialects versus national language is too strong here. See his *Nationalism and Language Reform in China* (Princeton: Princeton University Press, 1950), p. 53. Lutz's judgment that at least some Christian educators predicted "the vernacular would eventually replace classical Chinese as the literary language" seems more in keeping with the missionary record. See Jessie G. Lutz, *China and the Christian Colleges, 1850-1950* (Ithaca and London: Cornell University Press, 1971), p. 209.

19. The commission's recommendation was submitted in June 1911. See *Ch'ing-mo wen-tsu kai-ko wen-chi* [Documents on language

reform at the end of the Ch'ing period] (Peking: Wen-tzu kai-ko ch'u pan-she, 1958), pp. 116, 134, 143-44.

20. Li Chin-hsi, *Kuo-yü yün-tung shih-kang* [An outline history of the national language movement] (Shanghai: Commercial Press, 1935), pp. 11-12.

21. Ibid., p. 23; and Alfred Forke, "Neuere Versuche mit chinesischer Buchstabenschrift," *Mitteilungen des Seminars für Orientalische Sprachen* 9, part 1 (1906): 401-8.

22. An important contribution to clarifying the question is Milena Dolezelova-Velingerova's "The Origins of Modern Chinese Literature," in *Modern Chinese Literature in the May Fourth Era*, ed. Merle Goldman (Cambridge, Mass.: Harvard University Press, 1977), pp. 17-35.

23. Liang Ch'i-ch'ao, "Pien-fa t'ung-i" [On reform], in his *Yin-ping shih wen-chi* [Collected essays of Liang Ch'i-ch'ao] (Shanghai: Chung-hua ch'ien yin-pan, 1926), chüan 1, pp. 18a-34b; chüan 2, pp. 16a-60a.

24. Hu Shih, "Shih-ch'i nien-ti hui-ku," p. 5.

25. Liang Ch'i-ch'ao, "Lun hsiao-shuo yü ch'ün-chih chih kuan-hsi" [The relationship between fiction and democracy], in his *Yin-ping shih ho-chi*, vol. 4, part 1, p. 6. The essay was originally published in 1902.

26. Liang's views are recorded in "I-yin cheng-chih hsiao-shuo hsü" [On translating and publishing political fiction], in *Wan-ch'ing wen-hsüeh ts'ung-ch'ao, hsiao-shuo hsi-ch'ü yen-chiu chüan* [Collection of late Ch'ing literary documents, study of fiction and drama], ed. Ah Ying (Shanghai: Chung-hua, 1960), pp. 13-14. This essay was first published in 1898. See also Mabel Lee, "Liang Ch'i-ch'ao (1873-1929) and the Literary Revolution of Late Ch'ing," in *Search for Identity: Modern Literature and the Creative Arts in Asia*, papers presented to the 28th International Congress of Orientalists under the convenorship of Albert R. Davis (Sydney: Angus and Robertson, 1974), p. 204.

27. Robert W. Compton, "A Study of the Translations of Lin Shu, 1852-1924" (Ph.D. diss., Stanford University, 1971), p. 31.

28. Chang T'ai-yen (Ping-lin, 1869-1936) was a scholar and one of the most virulent anti-Manchuists. Like many other political activists, he had fled to Japan where he continued his political agitation and scholarly work.

29. Chou Tso-jen, *Chung-kuo hsin wen-hsüeh ti yüan-liu* [Sources for the new Chinese literature] (Peking: Jen wen-shu pu, 1934), preface dated 1932, p. 21. See also his *Yeh-tu-ch'ao* [Notes from night reading] (Shanghai: Pei hsin shu-shih, 1935), pp. 4-5, 7-8. Chou wistfully noted that had it not been for this literature he might have become a soldier or official.

30. Lu Hsün, "Mo-lo shih li shuo" [On the power of Mara poetry], in "Fen" [The grave (1907-25)], reprinted in *Lu Hsün san-shih nien-chi* [Lu Hsün's thirty-year collection] (Shanghai: Lu Hsün ch'üan chi ch'u pan-she, 1947), pp. 53-100.

31. Lu Hsün, "Wo tsen-mo tso-ch'i hsiao-shuo lai" [How I came to write fiction], in *Lu Hsün ch'üan-chi* [Collected works of Lu Hsün] (Shanghai: Lu Hsün ch'üan chi ch'u pan-she, 1946), 5:107. The essay was written in 1933.

32. Chou Tso-jen, trans., *YWHSC*, Introduction, p. 1.

33. Georg Brandes's *Poland, A Study of the Polish People and Literature* (London: William Heinemann, 1903) apparently served as the major source of information on Poland and Mickiewicz. The Chou brothers used the German Reclams Universal-Bibliothek series extensively for their translations. Chou Tso-jen expressed his special indebtedness to R. Nisbet Bain (1854-1909), whose translations from Hungarian, Russian, and Finnish fiction he had avidly read.

34. Clavin B. T. Lee, *The Campus Scene, 1900-1970, Changing Styles in Undergraduate Life* (New York: David McKay Co., Inc., 1970), pp. 13-44.

35. Professor Homer B. Hulbert suggested this in 1913 at Harvard and MIT. Hu Shih, then at Cornell, also showed an interest in the Korean system after being introduced to it by a friend. See *HSLHJC*, 1:270-80, 319-21. The entries are for 4 July 1914 and 15 September 1914.

36. Hu Shih, "Ch'ang-shih chi tzu-hsü" [Preface to *Collection of Experiments*], *HSWT*, 1:191.

37. Hu Shih recapitulated the development of the Literary Revolution in "Pi-shang liang-shan—wen-hsüeh ke-ming-ti k'ai shih" [Compelled to rebel—the beginning of the Literary Revolution], in *Chung-kuo hsin wen-hsüeh ta-hsi* [A corpus of China's new literature], ed. Chao Chia-pi (Hong Kong: Wen-hsüeh yen-chiu she, 1963, reprint ed.), 1:38-39, 41. Various entries from his student diary are also significant. See *HSLHJC*, 3: 844, entry dated 3 February 1916, and 3:826-66, entry dated 5 April 1916.

38. Apparently Hu had a passing acquaintance with Robinson prior to entering Columbia University in the fall of 1915. He mentions a visit with the James R. [sic] Robinson family in their summer home in Sheldrake in a letter to Miss Williams, dated 25 July 1915. At Columbia University he attended Robinson's classes.

39. These ideas are forcefully expressed in James H. Robinson's *The New History, Essays Illustrating the Modern Historical Outlook* (Springfield: The Walden Press, 1958).

40. Ch'en Tu-hsiu, "Wen-hsüeh ke-ming lun" [On literary revolution], *HCN* 2, no. 6 (February 1916): 487-88.

41. Richard C. Kagan, "From Revolutionary Iconoclasm to National Revolution: Ch'en Tu-hsiu and the Chinese Communist Movement," in *China in the 1920s, Nationalism and Revolution,* ed. F. Gilbert Chan and Thomas H. Etzold (New York: New Viewpoints, 1976), p. 59.

42. Hu Shih especially attacked Su Man-shu's fiction. See his "Ta Ch'ien Hsüan-t'ung shu" [Letter answering Ch'ien Hsüan-t'ung], *HSWT*, 1:41-45. The letter is dated November 1917.

43. Hu Shih, "The Chinese Literary Revolution," *Millard's Review* 8, no. 8 (19 April 1919): 277.

44. Chou Tso-jen, "Jen ti wen-hsüeh" [Human literature], in *TT*, 2:334-35. First published in *HCN* 5, no. 6 (December 1918): 575-84.

45. See especially Jaroslav Prusek, "A Confrontation of Traditional Oriental Literature with Modern European Literature in the Context of the Chinese Literary Revolution," *Archiv Orientalni* 32, no. 3 (1964): 365-75, and his Introduction to Marian Galik, *Mao Tun and Modern Chinese Literary Criticism* (Wiesbaden: Franz Steiner Verlag, 1969), pp. xi-xv.

46. Bonnie S. McDougall, *The Introduction of Western Literary Theories into Modern China, 1919-1925* (Tokyo: The Centre for East Asian Cultural Studies, 1971), pp. 54-55.

47. Galik, *Mao Tun and Modern Chinese Literary Criticism*, pp. 38, 77-79.

48. Mao Tun, *Hsüeh-jen* [The snowman] (Shanghai: Kaiming, 1929), p. 7.

49. Chao Chia-pi, ed., *Chung-kuo hsin wen-hsüeh ta hsi*, 10:82-83.

50. Lang Sun [Mao Tun], "Hsin wen-hsüeh yen-chiu-che ti tse-jen yü nu-li" [The tasks and efforts of researches in the field of new literature], *HSYP* 12, no. 2 (February 1921): 4.

51. Hu Shih, "Wu-shih nien-lai Chung-kuo chih wen-hsüeh" [Chinese literature in the past fifty years], *HSWT*, 2:180-261.

Chapter II Notes

1. Joseph T. Chen, *The May Fourth Movement in Shanghai, The Makings of a Social Movement in Modern China* (Leiden: E. J. Brill, 1971), pp. 14, 18.

2. See Irene Eber, "Thoughts on Renaissance in Modern China: Problems of Definition," in *Studia Asiatica*, ed. L. G. Thompson (San Francisco: Chinese Materials Center, Inc., 1975), pp. 189-218.

3. Hu Shih, "The Literary Renaissance," in *Symposium on Chinese Culture*, ed. Sophia H. Chen Zen (Shanghai: China Institute of Pacific Relations, 1931), p. 131.

4. *HSLHJC*, 3:784; entry dated 8 September 1915.

5. Chiang Mon-lin, "Kai-pien jen-sheng ti t'ai-tu" [Change our attitude toward life], in his *Kuo-tu shih-tai chih ssu-hsiang yü chiao-yü* [Thought and education in the transitional period] (Shanghai: Commercial Press, 1933), pp. 25-26; the article was first published in *Hsin chiao-yü* [New education], no. 5 (June 1919).

6. *HSLHJC*, 4:1151-53.

7. Wang Che-fu, *Chung-kuo hsin wen-hsüeh yün-tung shih* [A history of China's new literature movement] (Peiping: Ching-shan shu-she, 1933), pp. 29, 31.

8. Hu Shih, *The Chinese Renaissance* (New York: Paragon Book Reprint Corp., 1963), p. 46.

9. Hu Shih, "Renaissance in China," *Journal of the Royal Institute of International Affairs* 5 (November 1926): 265.

10. "Yin-yen" [Introduction], *HSYP* 12, no. 10 (October 1921): 5. This issue was dedicated to the literature of persecuted peoples *(pei-sun-hai min-tsu)*. "Wen-hsüeh hsün-k'an hsüan-yen" [Manifesto of the *Literary Ten Daily*], in *Chung-kuo hsin wen-hsüeh ta-hsi*, ed. Chao Chia-pi (Hong Kong: Wen-hsüeh yen-chiu she, 1963, reprint ed.), 10:82-83. Lu Hsün, "Chin-tai cheh-k'o wen-hsüeh kai-kuan" [A brief look at contemporary Czech literature], in *Lu Hsün i-wen chi* [Collection of Lu Hsün's translations] (Peking: Jen-min wen-hsüeh ch'u pan-she, 1958), 2:87. This essay first appeared in the October 1921 issue of *HSYP* under the pseudonym of T'ang Ssu. It is a translation from Joseph Karasek, *Slawische Literaturgeschichte* (Leipzig: G. J. Göschen'sche Verlagshandlung, 1906), 2 vols. Lu Hsün appended this statement to the translation.

11. Cheng Chen-to, "Ai-erh-lan ti wen-i fu-hsing" [Renaissance of Irish literature], in *Wen-hsüeh ta-kang* [Outlines of literature], ed. Cheng Chen-to (Shanghai: Commercial Press, 1927), 4:523. These and subsequent materials on Ireland are based in part on my earlier article "Chinese Views of Anglo-Irish Writers and Their Works in the 1920s," in *Modern Chinese Literature and its Social Context,* ed. Göran Malmqvist (Stockholm: Nobel Symposium no. 32, 1977), pp. 46-75.

12. Chou Yang, "Tui chiu hsing-shih li-yung tsai wen-hsüeh shang-ti i-ko k'an-fa" [A view on the utilization of old forms in literature], in *Chung-kuo hsien-tai wen-hsüeh shih ts'an-k'ao tzu-liao* [Materials for the study of modern Chinese literature] (Peking: Kao-teng chiao-yü ch'u pan-she, 1959), 1:734.

13. Cheng Chao-lin and Chu Sung-lu, trans., "Po-lan wen-hsüeh t'i-yao" [Important points of Polish literature], in *Hsüeh-i tsa-shih [Wissen und Wissenschaft]* 3, no. 10 (March 1922): 2-5. Emile Faguet, *Initiation Literaire* (Paris: Hachette, 1913).

14. Chou Tso-jen, "Chin-tai Po-lan wen-hsüeh k'ai-kuan" [Ideas on contemporary Polish literature], *HSYP* 12, no. 10 (October 1921): 9-12. Jan de Holewinski, *An Outline of the History of Polish Literature,* with a preface by G. P. Gooch (London: Published for the Polish Information Committee by G. Allen and Unwin, Ltd., 1916).

15. Chiba Kameo and Hai Ching, trans., "Po-lan wen-hsüeh ti t'e-hsing [Distinguishing features of Polish literature], *HSYP* 13, no. 7 (July 1922): 1-7.

16. Shen Yü, "Erh-shih nien-lai ti Po-lan wen-hsüeh" [Polish literature of the past twenty years], *HSYP* 20, no. 7 (July 1929): 1097.

17. [Chang] Wei-tz'u, "Ou-chou ti hsin kuo-chia: Po-lan" [Europe's new country: Poland], *Nu-li chou-pao* [Endeavour], no. 35 (31 December 1922): 1-3; no. 36 (7 January 1923): 2-3.

18. Wacław Borowy, "Fifteen Years of Polish Literature (1918-1933)," *Slavonic Review* 12 (1933-34): 670.

19. Lo Lo, "Po-lan chih fu-hsing" [Poland's revival], *TFTC* 16, no. 4 (April 1919): 63-70; and Chiba Kameo and Hai Ching, trans., "Po-lan wen-hsüeh ti t'e-hsing," p. 1.

20. Arthur P. Coleman, "Language as a Factor in Polish Nationalism," *Slavonic Review* 13, no. 37 (July 1934): 155-72.

21. Julian Krzyżanowski, *Neoromantyzm Polski, 1890-1918* [Polish neo-romanticism, 1890-1918] (Wrocław: Zakład Narodowy, 1971), pp. 9-26.

22. This is apparent from the bibliography list supplied by Ko Sui-ch'eng in his "Yu-t'ai jen-kou ti fen-pu ho chi min-tsu yün-tung ti kai k'uang" [The scattering of the Jewish people and their national movement], *TFTC* 26, no. 20 (October 1929): 113-23.

23. Heng-kai, "Ou-ch'an hou Yu-t'ai jen-min chih chüeh-wu" [The arousal of the Jewish people after World War I], *Min-hsin* [Popular sentiments] 1, nos. 34-35 (1919?); and Chün-shih, "Yu-t'ai jen chih wei-lai" [The future of the Jewish people], *TFTC* 15, no. 10 (October 1918): 44-55.

24. Ko Sui-ch'eng, "Yu-t'ai jen-kou ti fen-pu," p. 120. The source for this was Friedrich Wichtl, *Weltfreimaurerei, Weltrevolution, Weltrepublik* (Munich: J. F. Lehman, 1923).

25. "Yu-t'ai jen chih chih-yeh hsüeh-hsiao" [The Jews' professional schools], *Chiao-yü yü chih-yeh* [Education and professions] 57 (August 1924); and Yü K'an, "O-kuo Yu-t'ai jen ti i-chih yün-tung" [The migration movement of Jews in Russia], *TFTC* 25, no. 11 (June 1928): 3-5.

26. Yü Sung-hua, "Yu-t'ai jen yü Yu-t'ai fu-hsing yün-tung" [The Jews and the Jewish renaissance movement], *TFTC* 24, no. 17 (September 1927): 21-28.

27. This, as might be mentioned in passing, was apparently also Sun Yat-sen's view of the Zionist party, who called it "one of the greatest movements of the present time" in his letter addressed to Mr. N. G. B. Ezra, Shanghai, dated 24 April 1920, in the Zionist Archives, Jerusalem, MS Z4/10153.

28. Yü Sung-hua, "Pa-li-ssu-t'an ti-feng Ya-la-pa jen yü Yu-t'ai jen ti min-tsu yün-tung " [Palestine's Arab and Jewish national movements], *TFTC* 25, no. 8 (April 1928): 33-34.

29. Ko Sui-ch'eng, "Yu-t'ai jen-kou ti fen-pu," p. 121.

30. Yü Sung-hua, "Pa-li-ssu-t'an ti-feng Ya-la-pa jen yü Yu-t'ai jen ti min-tsu yün-tung," p. 30, and "Yu-t'ai jen yü Yu-t'ai fu-hsing yün-tung ," p. 25.

31. On this topic see the introduction by Arthur Hertzberg to his *The Zionist Idea, A Historical Analysis and Reader* (New York: Harper Torchbooks, 1966), pp. 15-100.

32. Louis D. Brandeis, "The Jewish Problem and How to Solve It," in ibid., pp. 517-23.

33. Ko Sui-ch'eng, "Hung-jen yü Hei-jen ti kai-k'uang chi ch'i min-tsu yün-tung" [Concerning Indians and blacks and their national movements], *TFTC* 26, no. 20 (October 1929): 147.

34. Tso-lin, "Mei-kuo ti fei-nu hsin yün-tung " [America's new slavery abolition movement], *TFTC* 23, no. 2 (January 1926): 60-63.

35. Yü K'an, "Hei-se-jen chung ti hsin chieh-fang yün-tung" [The new emancipation movement of American blacks], *TFTC* 23, no. 23 (December 1926): 66.

36. Ko Sui-ch'eng, "Hung-jen yü Hei-jen ti kai-k'uang chi ch'i min-tsu yün-tung," p. 158; and Yao Hsiung, "Mei-kuo ti Hei-jen wen-ti" [The question of American blacks], *TFTC* 24, no. 4 (February 1927): 50.

37. Ko Sui-ch'eng, "Hung-jen yü Hei-jen ti kai-k'uang chi ch'i min-tsu yün-tung," p. 160.

38. Yao Hsiung, "Mei-kuo ti Hei-jen wen-ti," p. 49.

39. Ibid., and Ko Sui-ch'eng, "Hei-jen ko tsu kai-k'uang chi ch'i kung-ho kuo chien-she yün-tung" [Concerning all black peoples and their movements of national reconstruction], *TFTC* 26, no. 7 (April 1929): 33.

40. Yü K'an, "Hei-se-jen chung ti hsin chieh-fang yün-tung," pp. 68-69.

41. The following is summarized from Nathan I. Huggins, *Harlem Renaissance* (New York and London: Oxford University Press, 1974), pp. 3, 22, 51, 58, 83.

42. On this topic see the provocative paper by Shalom Shai [Naomi Hazan], "Zionism and Pan-Africanism: Some Common Denominators," *ISS* (June 1976): 1-5.

43. Huggins, *Harlem Renaissance,* pp. 302-3.

44. Cheng Chen-to, "Ai-erh-lan ti wen-i fu-hsing," 4:523-40; and Shen Yen-ping, trans., "Hai-ch'ing ho-fu" [Hyacynth Halvey], HCN 9, no. 5 (September 1921): 27, appended note on Lady Gregory. Ernest A. Boyd, Ireland's Literary Renaissance (New York: John Lane Co., 1916). Frank W. Chandler, Aspects of Modern Drama (London: Macmillan, 1918).

45. Cheng Chen-to, "Ai-erh-lan ti wen-i fu-hsing," 4:523-24, 527, 535.

46. Liu Pan-nung, "Ai-erh-lan ai-kuo shih-jen" [Patriotic Irish poets], HCN 2, no. 2 (October 1916): 142-44.

47. "Ai-erh-lan shih-jen A. E. fang-wen chi" [A note of inquiry about the Irish poet A. E.], TFTC 19, no. 1 (January 1922): 100; and Shen Yen-ping, "Chin-tai wen-hsüeh ti fan-liu—Ai-erh-lan ti hsin wen-hsüeh" [A countercurrent in modern literature—Ireland's new literature], in Hsieh-shih chu-i yü langman chu-i [Realism and romanticism], comp. Wang Wen-ju (Shanghai: Commercial Press, 1925), p. 67.

48. Estella Ruth Taylor, The Modern Irish Writers, Cross Currents of Criticism (Lawrence: The University Press of Kansas, 1954), p. 5.

49. Huggins, Harlem Renaissance, pp. 201, 308.

50. Shen Yen-ping, "Po-lan chin-tai wen-hsüeh t'ai-tou Hsien-k'o-wei-chih" [Poland's contemporary notable writer Sienkiewicz], HSYP 12, no. 2 (February 1921): 1.

51. "Wen-hsüeh hsün-k'an hsüan-yen" [Manifesto of the Literary Ten Daily], in Chung-kuo hsin wen-hsüeh ta-hsi, ed. Chao Chia-pi, 10:82-83.

52. Shen Yen-ping, "Hsin Yu-t'ai wen-hsüeh kai-kuan" [Views on Yiddish literature], HSYP 12, no. 10 (October 1921): 65-66; and Cheng Chen-to, "Ai-erh-lan ti wen-i fu-hsing," 4:523.

53. Lang Sun [Mao Tun], "She-hui pei-ching yü ch'uang-tso" [Social background and creativity], HSYP 12, no. 7 (July 1921): 18.

54. For example, Yü Shang-yüan, "Chiu-hsi p'ing-chia [Evaluation of former drama], *CPFK* (1 July 1926): 3-6.

55. Shen Yen-ping, "Hsin Yu-t'ai wen-hsüeh kai-kuan," p. 61; Cheng Chen-to, "Ai-erh-lan ti wen-i fu-hsing," 4:530; "Ai-erh-lan shih-jen A. E. fang-wen chi," p. 100; and Chou Tso-jen, "Chin-tai Po-lan wen-hsüeh kai-kuan," pp. 9-12.

56. "Yin-yen," p. 2.

57. Note appended by Ku Te-lung to his translation "Po-chung jen" [The sowers], *HSYP* 16, no. 2 (February 1925): 4; and [Shen] Yen-ping, "Po-lan ti wei-ta nung-min hsiao-shuo chia Lai-mang-t'e [Poland's powerful peasant fiction writer Reymont], *WH* 155 (January 1925): 1. Hua Lu [Hu Yü-chih], "Tsai t'an-t'an Po-lan hsiao-shuo chia Lai-mang-t'e ti tso-p'in" [Another chat about the works of Poland's novelist Reymont], *WH* 156 (January 1925): 1-2. Fan Chung-yün, "Po-lan hsiao-shuo chia Lai-mang-te" [The Polish author Reymont], *TFTC* 22, no. 8 (April 1925): 110-15.

58. Shen Yen-ping, "Po-lan chin-tai wen-hsüeh t'ai-tou Hsien-k'o wei-chih," p. 4.

59. Julius Mrosik, *Das Polnische Bauertum im Werk Eliza Orzeszkowas* (München: Verlag Otto Sagner, 1963), p. 200.

60. Shen Yen-ping, "Chin-tai wen-hsüeh ti fan-liu—Ai-erh-lan ti hsin wen-hsüeh, " p. 38. Mao Tun's article is based largely on two chapters from Frank W. Chandler's *Aspects of Modern Drama*. The notion that this is a countercurrent, however, is Mao Tun's, and from time to time he adjusts the text accordingly.

61. [Shen] Yen-ping, "Chin-tai hsi-ch'ü chia ch'uan" [Biographies of contemporary playwrights], *Hsüeh-sheng tsa-chih* [The students' magazine] 6, no. 12 (December 1919): 106.

62. Yeh Ch'ung-chih, "Hsin-e (John M. Synge 1871-1909)," *CPFK* (1 July 1926): 1-4.

63. Wang T'ung-chao, "Hsia-chih ti sheng-p'ing chi-ch'i tso-p'in" [Yeats's life and works], *TFTC* 21, no. 2 (January 1924): 25, 39.

64. Cheng Chen-to, "I-chiu-erh-san nien No-pei-erh-chiang-chin che Hsia-chih" [The 1923 Nobel prize winner Yeats], *HSYP* 14, no. 12 (December 1923): 12. First published in *WHCP*, no. 97 (19 November 1923). Cheng's information on Yeats was based mainly on two volumes by Ernest A. Boyd, *Ireland's Literary Renaissance* and *The Contemporary Drama of Ireland* (Boston: Little, Brown, 1917). See also Cheng Chen-to, "Ai-erh-lan ti wen-i fu-hsing," 4:530.

65. "Ai-erh-lan shih-jen A. E. fang-wen chi," pp. 100, 103.

66. Hua Lu, "Tsai t'an-t'an Po-lan hsiao-shuo chia Lai-mang-t'e ti tso-p'in," p. 2.

67. Chao Ching-shen, "Hei-jen ti shih" [Black poetry], *HSYP* 19, no. 11 (November 1928): 1359.

68. Shen Yen-ping, "Yu-t'ai wen-hsüeh chia shih-shih" [Jewish writer about to die], *HSYP* 13, no. 11 (November 1922): 3; Shen Yen-ping and Cheng Chen-to, "Hsien-tai shih-chieh wen-hsüeh che lüeh-chuan" [Brief biographies of present-day world authors], *HSYP* 15, no. 3 (March 1924): 1-4; and Hai Ching, "Yu-t'ai wen-hsüeh yü Kao-pai-lin" [Jewish literature and Kobrin], *HSYP* 16, no. 12 (December 1925): 1.

69. Chiba Kameo and Han Ching [Mao Tun], trans., "Yu-t'ai wen-hsüeh yü Pin-ssu-ch'i" [Jewish literature and Pinski], *HSYP* 12, no. 7 (July 1921): 1-8.

70. Shen Yen-ping, "Hsin Yu-t'ai wen-hsüeh kai-kuan," pp. 61, 65-66.

71. Chao Ching-shen, "Hei-jen ti shih," p. 1359; Cheng Chen-to, "Ai-erh-lan ti wen-i fu-hsing," 4:537; and Yeh Ch'ung-chih, "Hsin-e," p. 4.

72. Huggins, *Harlem Renaissance*, p. 231.

73. Ch'i Ch'eng [Mao Tun], "Hsien-tai ti Hsi-pai-lai shih" [Modern Hebrew poetry], *HSYP* 14, no. 5 (May 1924): 1-7.

Chapter III Notes

1. Translations from Polish literature, most of which can be traced
   to their sources, provide good evidence. See Irene Eber,
   "Poland and Polish Authors in Modern Chinese Literature and
   Translation," *Monumenta Serica* 32 (1973): 407-45.

2. See the perceptive comments by Larry Sullivan and Richard H.
   Solomon, "The Formation of Communist Ideology in the May
   Fourth Era: A Content Analysis of Hsin Ch'ing Nien," in
   Ideology and Politics in Contemporary China, ed. Chalmers
   Johnson (Seattle and London: University of Washington Press,
   1973), pp. 134-40.

3. The debate is generally referred to as the controversy between
   science and a philosophy of life. It dealt with the question of
   what kind of philosophy would be most useful to develop in contemporary China. There were two broad groupings among intellectuals. One championed a rationalistic and scientific philosophy, and the other defended metaphysics. The essays on this
   topic are collected in Chang Chia-sen, Ting Wen-chiang, et. al.,
   K'o-hsüeh yü jen-sheng-kuan [Science and the philosophy of
   life], 2 vols. (Shanghai: Ya-tung, 1925).

4. Shen Yü, "Erh-shih nien-lai ti Po-lan wen-hsüeh," *HSYP* 20,
   no. 7 (1929): 1091-1100.

5. Patrick Hanan, "The Technique of Lu Hsün's Fiction," *Harvard
   Journal of Asian Studies* 34, (1974): 81.

6. For Ku's work, see Laurence A. Schneider, *Ku Chieh-kang and
   China's New History* (Berkeley, Los Angeles, London: University of California Press, 1971).

7. Shen Yen-ping, "Ai-erh-lan wen-t'an hsien-chuang chih i-pan"
   [A certain kind of present Irish literary scene], *HSYP* 12, no.
   5 (May 1921): 1-2.

8. Hsi Ti, trans., "Yin-tu yü-yen" [Indian fables], *HSYP* 15, no.
   11 (November 1924): 2.

9. Ibid., pp. 2-12, and *HSYP* 15, no. 12 (December 1924): 1-12.
   P. V. Ramaswami Raju, ed. and col., *Indian Fables* (London:
   Swan Sonnenschein Lowrey and Co., 1887).

10. Shen Yen-ping, "Po-lan chin-tai wen-hsüeh t'ai-tou Hsien-k'o-wei-chih," *HSYP* 12, no. 2 (February 1921): 2.

Chapter IV Notes

1. For a study of this group see Constantine Tung, *The Crescent Moon Society: The Minority's Challenge in the Literary Movement of Modern China* (State University of New York at Buffalo: Council on International Studies, 1972); Special Studies no. 11.

2. Marian Galik, "Die Tschechische und Slowakische Literatur in China (1919-1959)," *Asian and African Studies* (Bratislava) 6 (1970): 161-76. Galik mentions several Czech and Slovak translations, most of them from Esperanto sources.

3. Hua Lu [Hu Yü-chih], "Hsien shih-chieh jo-hsiao min-tsu chi-ch'i kai-k'uang" [Survey of the world's weak and small nations], *WH* 2, no. 5 (May 1934): 789.

4. Cheng Chang, *Shih-chieh jo-hsiao min-tsu wen-ti* [The problem of the world's oppressed peoples] (Shanghai: Chung-hua, 1940); first published in 1936.

5. Yang Jui-ling, "Ai-erh-lan tzu-yu pang-ti juo-ch'ü ho hsien-chuang" [The experiences of the Free Irish State and present affairs], *Shen-pao yüeh-k'an* [Shen-pao monthly] 3, no. 4 (15 April 1934): 67. Cheng Chang, *Shih-chieh jo-hsiao min-tsu wen-ti,* p. 203. "Ai-erh-lan tu-li yün-tung" [Ireland's independence movement], *Chung hsüeh-sheng tsa-chih* [The middle school student journal], no. 26 (July 1932): 8-11.

6. Cheng Chang, *Shih-chieh jo-hsiao min-tsu wen-ti,* pp. 157, 159. See also Yüan Ting-an, *Yu-t'ai chiao kai-lun* [A summary of Jewish teachings] (Shanghai: Commercial Press, 1935).

7. "Yu-t'ai jen tsai Pa-li-ssu-t'an tsung shih wen-hua chien-she" [Jews in Palestine are devoted to a cultural reconstruction], *WIYK* 4, no. 5 (November 1933): 176.

8. Wu Ch'ing-yu, "Yu-t'ai min-tsu wen-ti" [The problem of the Jewish people], *HCH* 4, no. 4 (February 1936): 7.

9. Margo S. Gewurtz, *Between America and Russia: Chinese Student Radicalism and the Travel Books of Tsou T'ao-fen, 1933-1937* (Toronto: University of Toronto, 1975), pp. 36-37.

10. Sheng Ch'eng, "Hei-jen-ti yin-yüeh" [Black music], *HCH* 4, no. 4 (July 1936): 63-64.

11. Note appended by Huang Yüan to his translation of chap. 17 of Walter White "Sui-shih li ti huo" [The fire in the flint], *WH* 1, no. 4 (October 1933): 586.

12. Langston Hughes, *I Wonder as I Wander: An Autobiographical Journey* (New York: Hill and Wang, 1964), p. 256. Lu Hsün likewise mentions meeting Hughes in his "Kei Wen-hsüeh she hsin [Letter to the Literature Society], in *Lu Hsün ch'üan chi* (Peking: Jen-min wen-hsüeh ch'u pan-she, 1957), 4:420-21. See also Donald C. Dickinson, *A Bio-Bibliography of Langston Hughes, 1902-1967* (Hamden, Conn.: Archon Books, 1967), pp. 117-19. Dickinson mentions a Japanese translation of *Not Without Laughter*, rather than a Chinese one. He also does not mention the Chinese translations of Hughes's poetry.

13. *WH* 1, no. 4 (October 1933): 586.

14. William E. B. DuBois, Herbert Aptheker, ed., *The Autobiography of W. E. B. DuBois: A Soliloquy on Viewing My Life from the Last Decade of its First Century* (New York: International Publishers, 1968), pp. 44-46.

15. For example, the importance of Paul Robeson's performance in *The Hairy Ape*. See "I-ko Hei-jen k'ou chung-ti Ao-ni-erh" [O'Neil via a black man], *TFTC* 29, no. 1 (January 1932): 41-42, or the notice of Hall Johnson's play *Run, Little Children, Run*, which was performed in New York in 1933. See also "Hei-jen Yüeh-Han-sun hsin tso hsi chü" [The black man Hall Johnson's new drama], *WIYK* 4, no. 2 (August 1933): 146.

16. "Ai-erh-lan wen-t'an hsin tung-hsiang" [New directions in Ireland's literature], *WH* 6, no. 4 (April 1936): 496.

17. "Ai-erh-lan shih-jen Hsia-chih chin-hsing" [Recent news on Ireland's poet Yeats], *WH* 4, no. 1 (January 1935): 157.

18. Fei Chien-chao, "Hsia-chih" [Yeats], *WIYK* 2, no. 1 (1931?): 13, 20.

19. Fei Chien-chao, "Ai-erh-lan tso-chia Ch'iao-ou-ssu" [The Irish author Joyce], *WIYK* 3, no. 7 (January 1933): 951-53.

20. Hsieh Sa, "Tsui-chin-ti Ai-erh-lan wen-t'an" [The most recent Irish literary scene], *HCH* 1, no. 15 (August 1933): 55-56. Kao Chih, "Ai-erh-lan wen-t'an" [Ireland's literary scene], *Wen-i*, no. 201 (21 August 1936): 14. Chao Ching-shen, "Tsui-chin-ti Ai-erh-lan wen-t'an" [The most recent Irish literary scene], *HSYP* 21, no. 9 (September 1930): 1412.

21. Tu Ch'eng-ssu, "Po-lan ming tso-chia— 1, Lai-mang-t'o, 2, Shen-lang-ssu-chi" [Famous Polish writers— 1, Reymont, 2, Zeromski], *WH* 2, no. 5 (May 1934): 806, 808.

22. Note appended to his translation by Sung Yung [Pu Ch'eng-chung], "Kuo-wang Ma-ch'i ti-i" [King Macius, the first], *WH* 4, no. 1 (January 1935): 162.

23. Chao Ching-shen, "Hsin Yu-t'ai tso-chia Na-ti-erh" [The Yiddish writer Nadir], *HSYP* 21, no. 11 (November 1930): 1675.

24. William Mulder, "The Uses of Adversity: The Literary Emancipation of the Black American," *Fulbright Newsletter*, Summer 1975, pp. 7-21.

25. George Brandon Saul, "A Wild Sowing: The Short Stories of Liam O'Flaherty," *Review of English Literature* 4 (July 1963): 108-13.

26. Korczak had served in the Russo-Japanese War and World War I. See Joseph Arnon, "The Passion of Janus Korczak," *Midstream* 19, no. 5 (May 1973): 32-53. Arnon attributes to Korczak the following statement, "War isn't murder. It's the victory parade of insane men coming home drunk from a Walpurgisnacht," ibid., p. 39.

116

27. For Joseph R. Levenson's comments on this play, see his *Revolution and Cosmopolitanism, The Western Stage and the Chinese Stages* (Berkeley: University of California Press, 1971), p. 41.

Chapter V Notes

1. Leszek Cyrzyk, "Książka Polska w Chinach" [The Polish book in China], *Twórczość* [Creativity] 14, no. 6 (1958): 161. Translation work carried out in the Republic of China since approximately 1950 is not considered in this study. For an excellent statistical analysis, see also Wolfgang Bauer, *Western Literature and Translation Work in Communist China* (Frankfurt/Main and Berlin: Alfred Metzner, 1964).

2. In, for example, Mao Tse-tung's *Talks at the Yenan Forum on Literature and Art* (Peking: Foreign Language Press, 1956); "On the Ten Major Relationships," in *Selected Works of Mao Tse-tung* (Peking: Foreign Language Press, 1977), 5:284-307; and *On the Correct Handling of Contradictions Among the People* (Peking: Foreign Language Press, 1957).

3. Marian Galik, "Die Tschechische und Slowakische Literatur in China (1919-1950)," *Asian and African Studies* (Bratislava) 6 (1970): 168.

4. See Irene Eber, "Old Issues and New Directions in Cultural Activities Since September 1976," in *Chinese Politics After Mao,* ed. Jürgen Domes (Short Hills, New Jersey: Enslow Publishers, n.d.).

5. *New China News Agency,* no. 6787 (27 October 1976): 15-16.

6. *New China News Agency,* no. 7321 (30 April 1978): 10.

7. Sun Wei, trans., "Po-lan jen-min ti ko-shou" [The singer of the Polish people], *IW,* no. 2 (May 1955): 109, 111.

8. "Lai-mang-t'e hsiao-shuo liang p'ien" [Two stories by Reymont], *IW,* no. 2 (February 1955): 238.

9. Wang Tso-liang, "Tang-tai Ai-erh-lan wei-ta ch'ü tso-chia Hsü-en Ao-k'ai-hsi" [Ireland's present-day great dramatist Sean O'Casey], *IW*, no. 2 (February 1959): 139, 141-44.

10. "Schiller and Shalom Aleichem Commemorated," *Peking Review*, no. 48 (12 January 1959): 20. The notice mentions the Chinese publication of Shalom Aleichem's *The Great Fair*. See also *Chinese Literature*, no. 2 (February 1960): 129, and *Der Tog* (9 September 1961): 2.

11. Ch'en Chen-kuang, "T'an Hsiao-lo-mu Ah-lai-han-mu ho ta ti tso-p'in" [On Shalom Aleichem and his works], *Chung-shan ta-hsüeh hsüeh-pao* [Sun Yat-sen University journal], nos. 1-2 (1959): 93-95.

12. Ch'en Chen-kuang, *Tsung shih-chi shang-lai* [The great fair] (Peking: Jen-min, 1959), p. 363.

13. Preface to *ICHHICK*, pp. 1-6. Note appended to his translation by T'ang Chen, "San-ko hsiao t'ou-erh" [Three little heads], *IW*, no. 7 (July 1957): 88.

14. Li Nien-p'ei, "I-ko chih-kung ti lüan ai" [A weaver's love], *IW*, no. 9 (September 1957): 105-6.

15. Mao Tse-tung, "Hu-hsü shih-chieh jen-min lien-ho ch'i-lai fan-tui Mei-kuo ti-kuo chu-i-ti ch'ung-tzu ch'i-shih, chih-ch'ih Mei-kuo Hei-jen fan-tui ch'ung-tzu ch'i-shih ti tou-cheng ti sheng-ming" [Calling upon the people of the world to unite to oppose racial discrimination by U.S. imperialism and support the American Negroes in their struggle against racial discrimination], *SCWH*, no. 9 (September 1963): 2-4. English translation appears in *Peking Review*, no. 33 (16 August 1963): 6-7.

16. Ping Hsing, "Tao Tu-po-i-ssu po-shi" [Grieving for Dr. DuBois], *SCWH*, no. 9 (1963): 18-21; and Liu Hui-ch'in, "Kuan-yü Lo-pai-t'e Wei-lien erh-san shih" [Several matters concerning Robert William], *SCWH*, no. 9 (September 1963): 5.

17. *Survey China Mainland Press*, no. 1957 (13 February 1959): 41; no. 1961 (17 February 1959): 35-36; no. 1962 (23 February 1959): 25-28; no. 1964 (21 February 1959): 45; no. 1965 (28 February 1959): 36. See also Yang Yü, "Dr. W. E. B. DuBois," *Chinese Literature* 5 (May 1959): 164-67.

18. Yeh Kuang, trans., "Mei-kuo wen-hsüeh chung-ti Hei-jen" [Blacks in American literature], *IW*, no. 5 (May 1959): 146-56.

19. Joseph R. Levenson, *Revolution and Cosmopolitanism, The Western Stage and the Chinese Stages* (Berkeley: University of California Press, 1971), pp. 7-8.

20. Ch'en Chen-kuang, *Tsung shih-chi shang-lai*, p. 363.

21. Douke W. Fokkema, *Literary Doctrine in China and Soviet Influence, 1959-1960*, (The Hague: Mouton and Co., 1965), pp. 166, 183, 236-38.

22. See Julius Mrosik, *Das Polnische Bauerntum im Werk Eliza Orzeszkowas* (München: Verlag Otto Sagner, 1963), p. 203.

23. Unfortunately few original works and even fewer translations were available to me. Particularly helpful for obtaining at least a cursory orientation regarding translations from Polish literature until 1955 was the bibliographical essay by Tadeusz Żbikowski, "O Przekładach literatury Polskiej w Chinach Ludowych" [Translation of Polish literature in the People's Republic of China], *Przegląd Orientalisticzny*, no. 2 (1955): 223-25.

24. I have not seen the Chinese translation of this novel, which was done in 1949. It is listed in Żbikowski's "O Przekładach literatury Polskiej," p. 223.

25. Listed in ibid. Liao Shang-kuo is given as the Chinese translator; the date of the Chinese translation is 1954.

26. Introduction to *ICHHICK*, pp. 4-5.

27. The Chinese anthology consists of a complete translation of a prior German translation containing the English originals, which was published in East Berlin. In the Chinese version, the appendix, which consists of brief biographical notices, is integrated into the text so that the biographies precede the poems.

28. Herbert Aptheker, *And Why Not Every Man?* (Berlin: Seven Seas Publishers, 1961).

29. See Tsi-an Hsia, "Twenty Years After the Yenan Forum," *The China Quarterly*, no. 13 (January-March 1963): 226-53.

Summary Notes

1. Yeh Shui-fu, "P'i-p'an 'wen-i hei hsien-chuan cheng' lun nu-li tso hao wai-kuo wen-hsüeh kung-tso" [Criticize the theory of "dictatorship of the sinister line in literature and art' and strive to make a success of the work on foreign literature], *Wen-hsüeh p'ing-lun* [Literature critic], no. 1 (February 1978): 48-52. Excerpts in *Foreign Broadcast Information Service*, no. 65, 4 April 1978.

2. Ibid., p. 49.

3. *Wai-kuo tuan-p'ien hsiao-shuo* [Foreign short stories] (Shanghai: Shanghai wen-hsüeh ch'u pan-she, 1978), 2 vols. In addition to German, English, French, and Japanese stories, this work also contains stories by Polish and Yiddish writers, among others.

APPENDIX A
CHRONOLOGICAL LISTING OF WORKS TRANSLATED BY
FIRST DATE OF APPEARANCE IN CHINESE

This year by year list of translated works from black American, Irish, Polish, and Yiddish literature is not definitive. Only those works that I have seen or that could be verified by multiple bibliographical listings have been included. Many references are unfortunately still incomplete because the available bibliographical resources did not supply sufficient information. Works that were reprinted in later publications or retranslated by another translator appear under the first and original entry. They are not cross listed under subsequent years of appearance. English titles are given according to published English translations whenever available, even when such titles do not conform to the original title or the Chinese version.

1909

Sienkiewicz, H.

1. a. Chou Tso-jen, "Ch'iu-ch'ang" [Sachem], in *YWHSC*, pp. 277-90.
   b. *HCN* 5, no. 4 (October 1918): 369-78.

2. a. Chou Tso-jen, "T'ien-shih" [Yamyol], in *YWHSC*, pp. 237-49.
   b. *HCN* 5, no. 4 (October 1918).
   c. [Wang] Lu-yen, in *HKWCHSC*.

3. a. Chou Tso-jen, "Lo-jen Yang-k'o" [Yanko the musician], in *YWHSC*, pp. 225-36.
   b. [Wang] Lu-yen, in *HKWCHSC*.

4. a. Chou Tso-jen, "Teng-t'ai tsung" [The lighthouse keeper of Aspinwall], in *YWHSC*, pp. 251-75.

122

b. Shih Chih-ts'un, "Teng-t'a shou" [The lighthouse keeper of Aspinwall], in *PLTPHSC*, 2:155-?

1919

Żeromski, S.

5. a. Mao Tun, "Yu-huo" [Temptation], *Hsüeh-teng* [School lamp] (December 1919).
    b. Chou Tso-jen, *HCN* 7, no. 3 (February 1920): 85-88.
    c. In *TT*, pp. 213-20.

1920

Gregory, A.

6. a. Wang Hsiao-yin, "Yüeh-shang" [The rising of the moon], *Hsin Chung-kuo* [New China] 2, no. 1 (15 January 1920).
    b. Ch'eng Tz'u-min, "Ming-yüeh tang-k'ung" [The rising of the moon], *CPFK*, no. 9, pp. 24-26.

Pinski, D.

7. a. Chou Tso-jen, "Pei-hsing wang-ch'üeh ti jen-min [Forgotten souls], *HCN* 8, no. 3 (November 1920): 427-38.
    b. In *KTK*, pp. 279-306.
    c. Wang Hsin-ch'ing, "Pei-wang chüeh ti ling-hun [Forgotten souls], *P'ing-min* [Plain people journal].

Żeromski, S.

8. a. Chou Tso-jen, "Huang-hun" [Twilight], in *TT*, pp. 221-36.
    b. *HCN* 7, no. 3 (February 1920): 89-94.

1921

Asch, S.

9. a. Shen Yen-ping, "Tung" [Winter], *HSYP* 12, no. 9 (September 1921): 24-33.
    b. In *HYTHSC*, pp. 43-68.

Asnyk, A.

10. Shen Yen-ping, "Wu-hsien" [Without limits], *HSYP* 12, no. 10 (October 1921): 105-6.

Gomulicki, W.

11.　　Chou Tso-jen, "Yen-tzu yü hu-tieh" [Swallows and butter-flies], *HSYP* 12, no. 8 (August 1921): 12-15.

12.　a.　Wang Ch'ien-san, "Nung-fu" [The ploughman], *HSYP* 12, no. 1 (January 1921): 28-30.
　　b.　In *PLWHIL*, vol. 1.

Gregory, A.

13.　　Shen Yen-ping, "Hai-ch'ing Ho-fu" [Hyacynth Halvey], *HCN* 9, no. 5 (September 1921): 1-27.

Konopnicka, M.

14.　a.　Chou Tso-jen, "Wo ti ku-mu" [My aunt], *HSYP* 12, no. 10 (October 1921): 1-8.
　　b.　In *PLWHIL*, vol. 1.

15.　　Shen Yen-ping, "Chin wang" [Now when the king], *HSYP* 12, no. 10 (October 1921): 104-5.

16.　　Chi Sheng, "Tuan-p'ien" [Fragments], *FNPL*, no. 16 (November 1921).

Peretz, Y. L.

17.　a.　Shen Yen-ping, "Fan-lai-chieh" [The fast], *HSYP* 12, no. 7 (July 1921): 7.
　　b.　In *HYTHSC*, pp. 1-10.
　　c.　In *HJ*.

Pinski, D.

18.　a.　Tung Fen [Mao Tun], "Mei ni" [The beautiful nun], *HSYP* 12, no. 8 (August 1921): 21-28.
　　b.　[Wang] Lu-yen, in *PSSC*.

Prus, B.

19.　a.　Chou Tso-jen, "Shih-chieh ti mei" [Lichens of the world], *HCN* 8, no. 6 (April 1921): 4-7.
　　b.　In *HTHSIT*, pp. 190-94.

20.　a.　Fei-pai, "Ying" [Shadows], *WHCP*, no. 3 (29 May 1921).
　　b.　Chou Tso-jen, *HSYP* 12, no. 8 (August 1921): 15-17.
　　c.　In *PLWHIL*, vol. 1.

Reymont, W.

21.　a.　Chung Ch'ih, "Shen-p'an" [The trial], *HSYP* 12, no. 2 (February 1921): 23-35.

124

b. Shih Chih-ts'un, in *PLTPHSC*.
c. In *PLWHIL*, vol. 1.

Shalom Aleichem

22. a. Shen Yen-ping, "Pei-no-ssu-hai-erh-ssu lai ti jen" [A man from Buenos Aires], *HSYP* 12, no. 10 (October 1921): 47-55.
    b. In *HYTHSC*, pp. 20-40.

Sienkiewicz, H.

23. a. Chou Tso-jen, "Erh-ts'ao-yüan" [Two meadows], *HSYP* 12, no. 9 (September 1921): 1-4.
    b. In *HTHSIT*.
    c. In *PLWHIL*, vol. 2.

24. a. Chou Tso-jen, "Yüan-ni yu fu-le" [Be blessed], *HCN* 8, no. 6 (April 1921): 839-42.
    b. Hsing Chen, "Hsü-shih ssu-fu-ti" [Be blessed], *CPFC* (1923).
    c. *Hsüeh-hui* [Learning fountain], no. 52.
    d. Sun Yung [Pu Ch'eng-chung], "Shou chu-fu-ti" [Be blessed], *IW* 2, no. 4 (1936): 890-94.

Szymanski, A.

25. a. Chou Chien-jen, "Yu-t'ai jen" [Srul— from Lubartow], *HSYP* 12, no. 9 (September 1921): 4-13.
    b. Chou Tso-jen, in *HTHSIT*, pp. 222-41.

Wendroff, Z.

26. a. Shen Tse-min, "Shu-la-k'o ho Po-la-ni" [Zerach and Bulani], *HSYP* 12, no. 6 (June 1921): 5-7.
    b. In *HYTHSC*, pp. 70-75.

Yeats, W. B.

27. Wang Ch'ien-san, "Jen-hsin" [An enduring heart], *HSYP* 12, no. 1 (January 1921): 32-33.

28. a. Fu Ch'üan, "Chiu-chih ke" [A drinking song], *Chüeh-wu* [Consciousness], no. 20 (September 1921).
    b. An I-hsüan, *HT* 1, no. 1 (May 1932): 26.

1922

Gregory, A.

29. Shen Yen-ping, "Lü-hsing jen" [The travelling man], *FNPL*, nos. 30 (1 March 1922) and 31 (8 March 1922).

30.   Shen Yen-ping, "Wu-ya" [The jackdaw], in *FNPL*, nos.
        34 (29 March 1922), 35 (5 April 1922), 36 (12 April 1922),
        37 (19 April 1922), and 44 (7 June 1922).

31.   Shen Yen-ping, "Yü-men" [The gaol gate], *FNPL*, nos.
        65 (1 November 1922) and 66 (8 November 1922).

Pinski, D.

32. a. Hsi Chen [Mao Tun], "La-pi Ah-ch'i-pa ti yu-huo"
         [Rabbi Akiba's temptation], *HSYP* 13, no. 1 (January
         1922): 26-32.
     b. In *HJ*.
     c. Wang Lu-yen, in *PSCC*.

33. a. Hsi Chen, "Po-lan—i-chiu i-chiu nien" [Poland 1919],
         HSYP 13, no. 9 (September 1922): 1-10.
     b. Wang Lu-yen, in *PSCC*.

34.   Hu Yü-chih, "Ts'an-fei che" [The cripples], *Min-to*
        [People's bell] 3, no. 2 (February 1922).

Prus, B.

35. a. Keng Shih-chih, "Ku Ai-ch'i ti chuan-shuo" [From the
         legends of ancient Egypt], *HSYP* 13, no. 3 (March 1922):
         45-51.
     b. In *PLWHIL*, vol. 2.

36. a. Hu Yü-chih, "Ta ai wo ma?" [Does she love me?], *TFTC*
         19, no. 15 (August 1922): 119-21.
     b. In *OCTLHSC*, pp. 43-46.

Sienkiewicz, H.

37. a. Chou Tso-jen, "Po-ni-k'o-la ti ch'in-shih" [Ponikla's
         organist], in *HTHSIT*, pp. 163-75.
     b. Hua K'an, "Hsing-chien ti i-shu chia" [Ponikla's
         organist], *Shih-chieh tsa-chih* [World journal] 2, no. 3
         (September 1931): 582-89.

Sieroszewski, W.

38. a. Li K'ai-hsien "Ch'iu-t'ien" [In autumn], *HSYP* 13, no.
         8 (August 1922): 13-24.
     b. In *PLWHIL*, vol. 2.

Zeissinger, H.

39. a. [Keng] Shih-chih, "Shu-lin chung ti sheng-tan-yeh"
         [Christmas night in the forest], *HSYP* 13, no. 2
         (February 1922): 43-46.
     b. In *PLWHIL,* vol. 2.

                              1923

Szymanski, A.

40.   Tung Ch'iu-fang, "I-ts'uo yen" [A pinch of salt],
          Chüeh-wu 9, no. 12 (August 1923).

Yeats, W. B.

41.   Wang T'ung-chao, "Wu tao-te ti meng ching" [Dreams
          that have no moral], *CPFC*, no. 2 (1923).

                              1924

Dunsany, E.

42.   Shen Yen-ping, "Ch'ien mao" [The lost silk hat], in
          HTTMC, pp. 49-67.

Gregory, A.

43.   Shen Yen-ping, "Shih-hu" [Spreading the news], in
          HTTMC, pp. 69-102.

Peretz, Y. L.

44. a. [Wang] Lu-yen, "Ling-hun" [What is the soul?], *TFTC*
         21, no. 11 (June 1924): 117-24.
     b. In *YTHSC.*

Pinski, D.

45. a. Ch'en Ku, "Pao feng-yü-li" [In the storm], *HSYP* 15,
         no. 3 (March 1924): 1-4.
     b. Wang Lu-yen, in *PSCC.*

46.   Hu Yü-chih, "Wai-chiao" [Diplomacy], in *HTTMC,* pp.
          83-155.

Shalom Aleichem

47. a. [Wang] Lu-yen, "La-pai-i-k'o" [Rabchik], *TFTC* 21, no.
         9 (May 1924): 107-15.

b. In *YTHSC*.

Sienkiewicz, H.

48. a. [Wang] Lu-yen, "Ch'üan-pien" [At the fountain], *HSYP* 15, no. 11 (November 1924): 1-4.
    b. In *HKWCHSC*.

Yeats, W. B.

49. Shen Yen-ping, "Sha-lou" [The hour-glass], in *HTTMC*, pp. 25-47.

50. Wang T'ung-chao, "Hsia-chih hsiao-p'in" [Short works by Yeats], *WHCP*, no. 105 (14 January 1924). Includes "Ku-chen" [The old town], "San-ko Ao-po-lun jen yü hsieh-mo" [The three O'Byrnes and the evil faeries], and "Sheng-yin" [A voice].

51. a. Chung Yün, "Lien-ai ti pei-ai" [The sorrow of love], *WHCP*, no. 104 (7 January 1924).
    b. An I-hsüan, "Lien-chih pei-ai" [The sorrow of love], *HT* 1, no. 1 (May 1932): 26.

52. Ch'ao Ching-shen, "Lao ma-ma ti ke" [The song of the old mother], *WHCP*, no. 109 (18 February 1924).

1925

Pinski, D.

53. a. Ch'en Ku, "I-ko o-jen ti ku-shih" [Tale of a hungry man], *HSYP* 16, no. 2 (February 1925): 1-14.
    b. Wang Lu-yen, in *PSCC*.

Reymont, W.

54. Ku Te-lung, "Po-chung jen" [The sowers], *HSYP* 16, no. 2 (February 1925): 1-14.

Shalom Aleichem

55. [Wang] Lu-yen, "Ho-hsia-no-la-p'o ti ch'i-chi" [The miracle of Hashono Rabo], *TFTC* 22, no. 15 (August 1925): 115-22.

Sienkiewicz, H.

56. a. [Wang] Lu-yen, "Chou-ssu-ti ts'ai-p'an" [The decision of Zeus], *HSYP* 16, no. 4 (April 1925): 1-4.

b. In *HKWCHSC*.

1926

Synge, J. M.

57.   Kuo Mo-jo, "Pei-ai-chih Tai-tai-erh" [Deidre of the sorrows], in *YHCKTHCC*.

58.   ———, "Hsi-ch'eng chih chien-erh" [The playboy of the Western world], in *YHCKTHCC*.

59.   ———, "Pu-kuo-chiang ti hun-li" [The tinker's wedding], in *YHCKTHCC*.

60.   ———, "Sheng ch'üan" [The well of saints], in *YHCKTHCC*.

61.   ———, "Ch'i-ma hsia-hai ti jen" [Riders to the sea], in *YHCKTHCC*.

62.   ———, "Ku-chung-ti an-ying" [The shadow of the glen], in *YHCKTHCC*.

1928

Asch, S.

63.   Tseng Hsü-pai, "Pei-ch'i che" [Abandoned], *Chen Mei Shan* [Truth, beauty, goodness] 1, no. 9 (March 1928): 1-10.

Prus, B.

64. a. Chu T'i-jan, "Hsin-ling tien-pao [Human telegraph], *Kung-hsien* [Contribution] 3, no. 1 (5 June 1928): 32-33.

    b. Shou Ts'an, "Jen ti tien-pao" [Human telegraph], *Kuo-wen chou-pao* [National news weekly] 5, no. 42 (28 October 1928): 1-2.

1929

Orzeszkowa, E.

65.   Chung Hsien-min, *Ma-erh-ta* [Martha] (Peking: Pei-hsin, 1929).

Shalom Aleichem

66.   Nan-ming [Chou Tso-jen], "Tz'u-pei" [A pity for the
       living], *Yü-ssu* [Fragments] 5, no. 12 (May 1929):
       647-56.

67.   ———— , "Ts'un-li ti Yü-yüeh-chieh" [Passover in a vil-
       lage], *Yü-ssu* 5, no. 13 (June 1929): 677-93.

                        1930

Prus, B.

68.   Tu Heng, *Shao-ping* [Outpost] (Shanghai: Kuang-hua,
       1930).

                        1931

Szymanski, A.

69. a. Shih Chih-ts'un, "Erh ch'i-tao che" [Two prayers],
        WIYK 2, nos. 11-12 (December 1931): 107-26.
     b. ———— , "Liang-ko ch'i-tao" [Two prayers], *PLTPHSC*,
        vol. 1, pp. 1-38.

                        1932

Yeats, W. B.

70.   An I-hsüan, "Hsia-chih shih-ch'ao" [Yeats's poetry],
       HT 1, no. 1 (May 1932): 23-27. Includes "Mu-yeh-
       chih tiao-ling" [The falling of the leaves], "Shui-chung
       hsiao-tao" [To an isle in the water], "K'o-erh-hu-shang
       chih yeh-fu" [The wild swans of Coole], "Ta hsi-wang-
       che t'ien-i" [He wishes for the clothes of heaven], and
       "Yin-ni-ssu-fu-li-chih hu-chou" [The lake isle of
       Innisfree].

                        1933

O'Flaherty, L.

71.   Su Ch'in-sun, "Ch'ing-lü" [The affectionate companion],
       WIYK 4, no. 3 (September 1933): 47-53.

White, W.

72.   Huang Yüan, "Sui-shih-li ti huo" [The fire in the flint],
WH 1, no. 4 (October 1933): 582-86.

1934

Hughes, L.

73.   Ku Feng, "Hei ti hua-huan" [Black garlands], *WH* 2, no.
5 (May 1934): 928-30. Includes "Kei hei-jen-nü" [Song
for a dark girl], "Ch'ang-kung" [Share croppers], and
"Shih-yüeh shih-liu" [October 16: the raid].

McKay, C.

74. a. Ku Feng, "Chia-ju wo-men pu-neng pu-szu" [If we must
die], included in "Hei ti hua-huan," *WH* 2, no. 5 (May
1934): 929.
    b. Chang Ch'i, in *HJSH*, p. 15.

Libin, S.

75.   Chao Chung-ch'ien, "Yeh-yen" [The picnic], *WH* 2, no. 5
(May 1934): 931-35.

Shalom Aleichem

76.   Huang I, "Yü-yüeh-chieh ti k'e-jen" [The Passover
guest], *WH* 2, no. 5 (May 1934): 936-40.

Tetmajer, K. P.

77. a. Fen Chün [Mao Tun], "Yeh-su ho ch'iang-tao" [Jesus
and the robbers], *WH* 2, no. 5 (May 1934): 804-6.
    b. Mao Tun, in *T'ao-yüan* [Peach grove] (Hongkong:
Chien-wen shu-chü, 1961); first published in 1935,
pp. 175-80.

Żeromski, S.

78.   Tu Cheng-ssu, "Tsai chia-pan-shang" [On deck of ship],
WH 2, no. 5 (May 1934): 807-8.

1935

Korczak, J.

79.   Sun Yung [Pu Ch'eng-chung], "Kuo-wang Ma-ch'i ti-i"
        [King Macius, the first], *WH* 4, no. 1 (January 1935):
        162-72.

Nomberg, H. D.

80.   Yin Yen, "Tsai shan-chung" [In the mountains], *Wen-
        hsüeh chi-k'an* [Literary quarterly] 2, no. 1 (July
        1935):   593-604.

O'Flaherty, L.

81.   Ling Tse-min, "Ch'iung-jen" [Poor people], *HCH* 3, no.
        6 (March 1935):   53-55.

82.   Chang Meng-lin, "Po-chung" [Spring sowing], *HCH* 3,
        no. 16 (1935):   53-56.

Sienkiewicz, H.

83.   Mao Tun, "Yu Mei tsa-chi" [Notes from an American
        journey], in Cheng Chen-to, ed., *Shih-chieh wen-k'u*
        [World treasury of literature] (Shanghai: Sheng-huo,
        1935), 2:575-883.

1936

Asch, S.

84.   T'ang Hsü-chih, *Fu-ch'ou-shen* [The God of vengeance]
        (Shanghai: Commercial Press, 1936).

Kaden-Bandrowski, J.

85.   Shih Chih-ts'un, "Ssu-hsing p'an-chüeh" [The sen-
        tence], in *PLTPHSC*, 2:101-45.

Nałkowska-Rygier, Z.

86.   Shih Chih-ts'un, "Tz'u-hsing" [Farewell], in *PLTPHSC*,
        1:39-51.

O'Faolain, S.

87.   Hsü T'ien-hung, "Su-li-wen ti ku-tzu" [Sullivan's
        trousers], *IW* 1, no. 5 (1936):969-92.

O'Flaherty, L.

88.   Yüeh Wen [Chou Shu-jen?], "I-ko hsien-ling" [A shilling], *HCH* 4, no. 11 (July 1936):61-62.

Orzeszkowa, E.

89.   Shih Chih-ts'un, "Ni chi-te ma?" [Do you remember?], *PLTPHSC*, 2:147-54.

Sienkiewicz, H.

90.   Chou Tso-jen, *T'an-hua* [Charcoal sketches] (Peking: Pei-hsin, 1936).

Sieroszewski, W.

91.   Shih Chih-ts'un, "Ch'iao-k'o-ch'ieh jen" [The Chukchi people], in *PLTPHSC*, 1:53-99.

Żeromski, S.

92.   Shih Chih-ts'un, "Ch'iang-ti hsing" [The stronger sex], in *PLTPHSC*, 2:179-216.

1941

Peretz, Y. L.

93.   Chi Chen-po, "Mu-ch'in" [Mother], *Chieh-fang jih-pao* [Liberation daily], no. 254 (28 January 1941), p. 3; no. 256 (29 January 1941), p. 3; and no. 260 (2 February 1941), p. 3.

1942

Peretz, Y. L.

94.   Chi Chien-po, "P'eng-ch'i. Sai-lin-t'e [Bontshe the silent], *Chieh-fang jih-pao*, no. 295 (9 March 1942), p. 3 and no. 296 (9 March 1942), p. 3.

1943

Clarke, D.

95.   Fang Ching, "Chi-o" [Starvation], *Wen-hsüeh i-pao* [Literature translations] 1, no. 5 (1943): 72-79.

1944

Wright, R.

96.   Huang Sung-ch'i, *Hei hai-tzu* [Native son] (Tso-chia, 1944).

1945

Wasilewska, W.

97.   Ts'ao Ching-hua, *Hung* [Rainbow] (Chang-chia-kou: Hsin-hua, 1945).

1947

Wright, R.

98.   Yü Huai-cheng, *Hsiao hei-jen* [Black boy] (Ta-t'ung, 1947).

1950

Wasilewska, W.

99.   Chin Jen, *Chih pu-kuo shih ai-ch'ing* [This is simply love] (Peking: Hsin-hua, 1950).

1953

Prus, B.

100.   Hai Kuan, "Mi-ho-erh-k'o" [Michalko], *IW*, no. 12. (December 1953), pp. 51-79.

Kruczkowski, L.

101. a. Li Chien-wu, *Lo-sen-p'u fu-fu* [Julius and Ethel] (Shanghai: Hsin-wen-i, 1954).
      b. P'ing Tsun-ping, *Lo-sen-p'u fu-fu* (Peking: Tso-chia, 1955).

Prus, B.

102.   Hai Kuan, "Hui lang" [The returning wave], *IW*, no. 6 (June 1954), pp. 33-113.

103.   Chuang Shu-tz'u, "I-chien pei-hsin" [The vest], *IW*, no. 6 (June 1954), pp. 114-25.

Rudnicki, A.

104.   Ling Shan, "Yüeh-se-fu" [Josefòw], *IW*, no. 3 (March 1954), pp. 104-16.

Sienkiewicz, H.

105.   Shih Chih-ts'un, "Ao-erh-so" [Orso], *IW*, no. 1 (January 1954).

106.   Wang I, "Wei-le mien-pao" [For bread], *IW*, no. 1 (January 1954), pp. 127-29.

1955

Reymont, W.

107.   "T'ang-mei-k'o Pa-lan" [Tomek Baran], *IW*, no. 2 (February 1955), pp. 180-234.

108.   Shih Chih-ts'un, "Szu" [Death], *IW*, no. 2 (February 1955), pp. 155-79.

1957

Anonymous (Folksongs)

109.   Chang Ch'i, "Ma-li-ah, pieh k'u-la" [Oh Mary, don't you weep], in *HJHS*, pp. 92-93.

110.   ————, "Min-ke (1853)", [Song 1853], in *HJHS*, p. 97.

111.   ————, "Min-ke (1859)", [Song 1859], in *HJHS*, p. 98.

112.   ————, "Nu-li ti so-lien" [Slavery chains], in *HJHS*, pp. 90-91.

113.   ————, "Shih-hui-fei shih wo yu-yü [Silicosis blues], in *HJHS*, pp. 101-2.

114.   ————, "Ta tsung pu pao-yüeh" [He never said a mumbaling word], in *HJHS*, pp. 88-89.

115.   ————, "Wo ho wo ti shang-szu" [Me and my captain], in *HJHS*, pp. 99-100.

116. Chang Ch'i, "Yao-shih wo neng sui hsin-so-yüan" [If I had my way], in *HJHS*, pp. 94-96.

Brown, S. A.

117. Chang Ch'i, "Nan-fang ti tao-lu" [Southern road], in *HJHS*, pp. 42-45.

118. ————, "Lao Lai-mu" [Old Lem], in *HJHS*, pp. 46-49.

119. ————, "Chien-ch'iang ti jen-min"[Strong men], in *HJHS*, pp. 50-54.

Cotter, J. S.

120. Chang Ch'i, "Ni yao shuo shih-ma?" [And what shall you say?], in *HJHS*, pp. 9-10.

Cullen, C.

121. Chang Ch'i, "Hsieh yü hei-t'a [From the dark tower], in *HJHS*, pp. 17-18.

Cuney, W.

122. Chang Ch'i, "Chao pu chien shen-ying" [No images], in *HJHS*, pp. 36-37.

Dąbrowska, M.

123. Ya-k'o, Ch'eng-ch'iu, "Hsiang-ts'un hun-li" [A village wedding], *IW*, no. 10 (October 1957), pp. 3-53.

Davis, F. M.

124. Chang Ch'i, "Nan-fang ch'an-mien-ch'ü ti hua-hsing" [Snapshots of the cotton south], in *HJHS*, pp. 55-56.

Dunbar, P. L.

125. Chang Ch'i, "Wo-men tai-che chia-mien-chü" [We wear the mask], in *HJHS*, pp. 7-8.

Harper, F. E. W.

126. Chang Ch'i, "Jang kuang-ming chin-lai" [Let the light enter], in *HJHS*, pp. 5-6.

Hayden, R.

127. Chang Ch'i, "Yü-yen" [Prophecy], in *HJHS*, pp. 76-77.

128. ————, "Chia-pu-jui-erh" [Gabriel], in *HJHS*, pp. 78-80.

136

129.   Chang Ch'i, "Yen-shuo [Speech], in *HJHS*, pp. 81-82.

Horne, F.

130.   Chang Ch'i, "Hei-jen jen" [Nigger], in *HJHS*, pp. 38-41.

Horton, G. M.

131.   Chang Ch'i, "Wo" [Myself], in *HJHS*, pp. 1-2.

Hughes, L.

132.   Chang Ch'i, "Hei-jen t'an ho-liu" [The Negro speaks of rivers], in *HJHS*, pp. 21-23.

133.   ————, "T'ung-t'an-yü" [Brass spittoons], in *HJHS*, pp. 24-26.

134.   ————, "T'i i-ko hei-jen-ku-niang tso-ti ke" [Song for a dark girl], in *HJHS*, p. 27.

135.   ————, "Jang Mei-kuo chung-hsin-ch'eng wei Mei-kuo" [Let America be American again], in *HJHS*, pp. 28-33.

136.   ————, "Wo ye ke-ch'ang Mei-kuo" [I too sing America], in *HJHS*, pp. 34-35.

Johnson, F.

137.   Chang Ch'i, "Yen-chüan" [Tired], in *HJHS*, pp. 11-12.

McKay, C.

138.   Chang Ch'i, "Mei-kuo" [America], in *HJHS*, p. 13-14.

139.   ————, "Ssu-hsing" [The lynching], in *HJHS*, p. 16.

O'Casey, S.

140.   Chu-yen, "Hsing-hsing pien hung-le" [The star turns red], *IW*, no. 2 (February 1959), pp. 80-113.

Orzeszkowa, E.

141.   Shih Yu-sung, "Huang-nien" [Years of draught], *IW*, no. 6 (June 1957), pp. 63-74.

Peretz, Y. L.

142.   Li Nien-p'ei, "I-ko chih-kung ti lüan-ai" [A weaver's love], *IW*, no. 9 (September 1957), pp. 92-105.

143.   Hsi Tzu, "Sung-hsin jen" [The messenger], *IW*, no. 9 (September 1957), pp. 85-92.

144.   ————, "Ch'ien-ch'eng ti miao" [The devout cat], *IW*, no. 9 (September 1957), pp. 83-84.

Shalom Aleichem

145.   T'ang Chen, "Yung-sheng" [Eternal life], *IW*, no. 7 (July 1957), pp. 67-83.

146.   T'ang Chen, "San-ko hsiao t'ou-erh" [Three little heads], *IW*, no. 7 (July 1957), pp. 83-88.

Tolson, M. B.

147.   Chang Ch'i, "Hei-se chiao hsiang-yüeh" [Dark symphony], in *HJHS*, pp. 67-75.

Toomer, J.

148.   Chang Ch'i, "Ta-ti-jen tzu-chih ke" [Song of the son], in *HJHS*, pp. 19-20.

Walker, M.

149. a. Chang Ch'i, "Wei-le wo ti jen-min" [For my people], in *HJHS*, pp. 83-85.

    b. ————, *IW*, no. 5 (May 1959), p. 156.

Whitfield, J. M.

150.   Chang Ch'i, "Mei-kuo" [America], in *HJHS*, pp. 3-4.

1958

Broniewski, W.

151.   P'ei Yüan-ying, "Shih liu shou" [Poetry in six stanzas], *IW*, no. 3 (March 1958), pp. 134-39.

1959

Shalom Aleichem

152.   Chou Tso-t'o, "Shih-kuai ming-chien" [Menahem Mendel, agent], in *ICHHICK*, pp. 1-16.

153.   Ch'en Chen-kuang, "I-ch'ang huan-hsi i-ch'ang k'ung" [Poor and happy], in *ICHHICK*, pp. 17-43.

154.   Ch'en Chen-kuang, "Chiao-ju wo shih Lo-hsi-erh" [If I were Rothschild], in *ICHHICK*, pp. 44-50.

155. a. Chang Lu-pei, "Tao-mei ti jen" [Bad luck], in *ICHHICK*, pp. 51-58.
      b. [Wang] Lu-yen, in *YTHSC*.

156.   Chu Lin-ming, "Shen-hsüeh chiao-shih Po-i-ah-ssu" [Boaz the teacher], in *ICHHICK*, pp. 59-72.

157.   ?, "Ma-t'u-sa-la" [Methusala], in *ICHHICK*, pp. 73-90.

158.   Huang Cho-han, "Yüeh-se-fu" [Joseph], in *ICHHICK*, pp. 91-122.

159.   Ch'en Chen-kuang, "Ya-k'o" [The Song of Songs], in *ICHHICK*, pp. 123-200.

160.   ————, *Tsung shih-chi-shang lai* [The great fair] (Peking: Jen-min, 1959).

161.   T'ang Chen, "I-pao huan i-pao" [Tit for tat], *SCWH*, no. 3 (March 1959), pp. 86-96.

1961

Wygodski, S.

162.   Hsieh Hsin-hui, "Hui-chien" [Meeting], *SCWH*, no. 12 (December 1961), pp. 23-42.

1962

Prus, B.

163.   Ch'ing Yüan, "An-t'ai-k'o" [Antek], *SCWH*, no. 5 (May 1962), pp. 2-25.

1963

Copeland, J. A.

164.   Hsia Ch'ing, "Kei hsiung-ti ti i-shu" [Last words of a Negro who died with John Brown], *SCWH*, no. 9 (September 1963), pp. 218-19.

Douglass, F.

165.   Hsia Ch'ing, "Hei-jen-min, ts'an chün-pa!" [Men of
color, to arms!], *SCWH*, no. 9 (September 1963), pp.
98-100.

DuBois, W. E. B.

166.   Ping Hsin, "Chia-na tsai chao-huan" [Ghana calls],
SCWH, no. 9 (September 1963), pp. 13-17.

Garnet, H. H.

167.   Hsia Ch'ing, "Ch'i-ti hao chao" [A public call for rebel-
lion], *SCWH*, no. 9 (September 1963), pp. 95-96.

Luce, P. A.

168.   Pu Chih, "Hsien-kei Ma-k'o. Pa-k'o-erh" [Mack
Parker], *SCWH*, no. 9 (September 1963), pp. 26-28.

Walker, M.

169.   Ching Wen [Chung Ching-wen], "Pei-shan ti ku-hsiang"
[Sorrow home], *SCWH*, no. 9 (September 1963), pp.
29-30.

Williams, J.

170.   Wen-lan, "Ch'un-t'ien [Spring], *SCWH*, no. 9
(September 1963), pp. 24-25.

Uncertain Dates, the 1920s

Peretz, Y. L.

171.   [Wang] Lu-yen, "Tzu-mei" [Sisters], in *YTHSC*.

172.   ———, "Ch'i-nien hao-yün" [Seven years of plenty],
in *YTHSC*.

173.   ———, "Ho-erh-mu-ssu yü Ah-ssu-man" [Ormuzd and
Ahriman], in *YTHSC*.

174.   ———, "P'i-ts'ang hsieh-piao-mu" [Pidjon Shwuim],
in *YTHSC*.

Pinski, D.

175.   [Wang] Lu-yen, "Pan-yün-fu" [The porter], in *YTHSC*.

Shalom Aleichem

176.   [Wang] Lu-yen, "Chung-hsüeh hsiao" [Gymnazya], in
         YTHSC.

177.   ————, "Pao" [The treasure], in *YTHSC*.

178.   ————, "Ch'uang-tsao nü-jen ti ch'uan-shuo" [A
         woman's wrath], in *YTHSC*.

Sienkiewicz, H.

179.   [Wang] Lu-yen, *Ti-chung hai-pin* [Bright shores].

180.   Hsü Ping-ch'ang and Ch'iao Ts'eng-min, *Ni wang ho
         ch'u-chu* [Quo vadis] (Shanghai: Commercial Press,
         n.d.).

181.   Yeh Ling-feng, *Meng-ti-chia-lo* [Monte Carlo] (Shanghai:
         Kuang-hua, n.d.).

APPENDIX B
WORKS FROM WHICH CHINESE TRANSLATIONS WERE PREPARED

The numbers in brackets following each entry refer to the translated items as listed in Appendix A.

Aptheker, Herbert. *And Why Not Every Man?* Berlin: Seven Seas Publishers, 1961. [164, 165, 167]

Benecke, Else C. M., trans. *Tales by Polish Authors.* Oxford: B. H. Blackwell, 1915. [5bc, 8ab, 38a]

Benecke, Else C. M., trans. *More Tales by Polish Authors.* New York: Longmans Green, 1916. [21ab, 92, 102]

Benecke, Else C. M., and Busch, Marie, trans. *Selected Polish Tales.* London and New York: Oxford University Press, 1925. [40, 68, 85, 86, 108]

Berman, Hannah, trans. *Jewish Children. From the Yiddish of "Shalom Aleichem".* New York: Alfred A. Knopf, 1922. [66, 67]

Clark, Barret H., and Lieber, Maxim, eds. *Great Short Stories of the World.* Cleveland and New York: The World Publishing Co., 1925. [63, 177]

Clark, Barret H., and Lieber, Maxim, eds. *Great Short Stories of the World.* New York: Robert M. McBride and Co., 1928. [75, 76]

Curtin, Jeremiah, trans. *Sielanka: A Forest Picture and Other Stories.* Boston: Little Brown and Co., 1898. [1ab, 2ab, 3a, 4a, 56a]

Dunsany, [Lord] Edward. *Five Plays.* New York: A. Mitchell Kennerly, 1914. [42]

Freedomways 2, no. 1 (Winter 1962): 71-74, 95-96; no. 2 (Spring 1962): 160. [166, 168, 170]

142

Goldberg, Isaac, trans. *David Pinski. Ten Plays.* New York:
B. W. Huebsch, 1920. [18a, 33a, 34, 46]

Goldberg, Isaac, trans. *Temptations, A Book of Short Stories by
David Pinski.* London: George Allen and Unwin, Ltd., 1919.
[32, 45, 53]

Goldberg, Isaac, trans. *Six Plays of the Yiddish Theatre.*
Boston: John W. Luce and Co., 1916. [7ab, 9]

Grabowski, A., trans. *Antologio Internacia.* France: Hatchette,
1904. [19a, 24a]

Gregory, [Lady] Augusta. *Seven Short Plays.* New York and
London: G. P. Putnam's Sons, 1915. [6ab, 13, 29, 30, 31,
43]

Hermlin, Stephen, trans. *Auch Ich Bin Aus Amerika, Dichtungen
Amerikanischer Neger.* Berlin: Verlag Volk und Welt, 1948.
[109-122, 124-139, 147-150]

*"Jewish Life" Anthology, 1946-1956. A Selection of Short Stories,
Poems and Essays Drawn from the Magazine.* Compiled by
the Editorial Board of *Jewish Life.* New York: Progressive
Jewish Life, Inc., 1956. [142]

Kabe [Kazimierz Bein], trans. *Pola Antologio.* France:
Hatchette, 1906. [11a, 14a, 20a, 23ab, 36a]

Literatura Mondo Kuars Kvius Numero [World literature].
Hungary, May-June 1935. [80]

O'Casey, Sean. *Collected Plays.* London: Macmillan Co., Ltd.,
1952. [140]

O'Flaherty, Liam. *Spring Sowing.* London: Butler and Tanner,
Ltd., 1927. [82]

O'Flaherty, Liam. *The Tent.* London: Jonathan Cape, 1926.
[88]

Salom-Alehem, Perec, Mučnik, Is., trans. *Hebreaj Rakontoj.*
Leipzig: Ferdinand Hirt und Sohn, 1923. [47, 55, 171,
173, 174, 177]

Selver, Paul. *Anthology of Modern Slavonic Literature in Prose
and Verse.* London: Kegan-Paul, Trench, Trubner and
Co., Ltd., 1919. [10, 12ab, 15, 35ab]

Sennacieca Revuo 1, no. 12 (December 1933). [143]

White, Walter F. *The Fire in the Flint*. New York: Alfred A. Knopf, 1924. [72]

Wright, Richard. *Black Boy. A Record of Childhood and Youth.* Cleveland and New York: The World Publishing Co., 1937. [98]

Wright, Richard. *Native Son.* New York and London: Harper and Brothers Publishers, 1940. [96]

Yeats, William Butler. *Celtic Twilight.* London: A. H. Bullen, 1902. [27]

Yeats, William Butler. *The Hour-Glass and Other Plays. Being Volume Two of Plays for an Irish Theatre.* New York: The Macmillan Co., 1906. [49]

Żołtowska, S., trans. "The Sowers." *The Slavonic Review* 3, no. 7 (June 1924): 37–45. [54]

APPENDIX C
BIOGRAPHICAL LISTING OF AUTHORS
WHOSE LITERARY WORKS WERE TRANSLATED

A. E. (1867-1935)
   Pseudonym of George William Russell. Irish literary figure and poet.

Andrzejewski, Jerzy (b. 1909)
   Polish writer, active in underground during World War II.

Asch, Sholem (1880-1957)
   Major Yiddish novelist and playwright.

Asnyk, Adam (1830-1897)
   Polish poet.

Broniewski, Władisław (1896-1962)
   Polish poet and translator.

Brown, Sterling A. (b. 1901)
   Black poet.

Clarke, Desmond (b. 1907)
   Irish short story writer and librarian.

Copeland, John A.
   Black.

Cotter, Joseph Seamon, Jr. (1895-1919)
   Black poet.

Cullen, Countee (1903-1946)

   Black poet and leading figure in the Harlem Renaissance.

Cuney, Waring (b. 1906)
   Black poet.

Dąbrowska, Maria (1889-1965)
   Polish writer well known for her village portraits.

Davis, Frank Marshall (b. 1905)
Black poet.

Douglass, Frederick (1817-1895)
Black.

DuBois, William E. B. (1868-1963)
One of the most influential and prominent black leaders of the twentieth century. Active in political, intellectual, and literary life.

Dunbar, Paul Laurence (1872-1906)
First major black poet with a national reputation.

Dunsany, [Lord] Edward (1878-1957)
Pseudonym of Edward John Moreton Drax Plunkett. Irish playwright and fiction writer.

Garnet, Henry Highland (1815-1882)
Black writer.

Gomulicki, Wiktor (1850-1919)
Polish writer and poet.

Graham, Shirley (b. 1904)
Black historian, biographer, and dramatist. Wife of William E. B. DuBois.

Gregory, [Lady] Augusta (1852-1932)
Irish nationalist and dramatist. Major figure in the Literary Revival and moving force in the Irish theatre.

Harper, Frances E. W. (1825-1911)
Black writer and poet.

Hayden, Robert (b. 1899)
Black poet.

Horne, Frank (b. 1899)
Black poet.

Horton, George Moses (1797-1883)
Black poet.

Hughes, Langston (1902-1967)
Major black literary figure in the Harlem Renaissance and thereafter.

Johnson, Fenton (1888-1958)
Black poet.

Kaden-Bandrowski, Juliusz (1885-1944)
    Polish writer killed during the Warsaw uprising.

Konopnicka, Maria (1842-1910)
    Polish poet and short story writer. Active as social reformer
    and nationalist.

Korczak, Janusz (1877-1942)
    Pseudonym of Henryk Goldszmit. Jewish educator and
    writer murdered during World War II.

Kruczkowski, Leon (1900-1962)
    Polish author and dramatist. He was especially active in
    cultural and publishing circles after 1945.

Libin, Solomon (1872-1955)
    Pseudonym of I. Hurwitz. Yiddish writer especially of New
    York Jewish life.

Luce, Phillip Abbott (b. 1938)
    Black writer.

McKay, Claude (1890-1948)
    Major black writer and poet.

Nałkowska, Zofia (1885-1954)
    Polish novelist well known for her feminine portrayals.

Nomberg, Hirsch David (1876-1927)
    Modern Jewish author of Hebrew and Yiddish works.

O'Casey, Sean (1880-1964)
    Contemporary radical Irish writer and dramatist.

O'Faolain, Sean (b. 1900)
    Irish author.

O'Flaherty, Liam (b. 1896)
    Popular Irish writer.

Orzeszkowa, Eliza (1841-1910)
    Major Polish writer who championed social justice and equal
    rights, and criticized social backwardness.

Peretz, Yitzchak Leib (1851-1915)
    Literary master of major influence on Yiddish writers.

Pinski, David (1872-1959)
    Major Yiddish dramatist, novelist, and editor.

Prus, Bolesław (1845-1912)
Pseudonym of Alexander Głowacki. Major Polish writer and
exponent of the realist school.

Reymont, Władisław Stanisław (1867-1925)
Major Polish writer and Nobel Prize winner in 1924.

Rudnicki, Adolf (b. 1912)
Polish writer of Jewish origin. His major works since World
War II deal with Nazi crimes against Polish Jews.

Shalom Aleichem (1859-1916)
Pseudonym of Sholem Rabinovitch. Satirist, humorist, and
major Yiddish writer often compared to Mark Twain.

Sienkiewicz, Henryk (1846-1916)
Most important Polish literary figure of the nineteenth century and Nobel Prize winner in 1905.

Sieroszewski, Wacław (1858-1945)
Polish novelist and short story writer known for his descriptions of Siberian exile.

Synge, John Millington (1871-1909)
Major Irish playwright.

Szymanski, Adam (1852-1916)
Polish novelist known for his fiction about Polish exiles in
Siberia.

Tetmajer, Kazimierz Przerwa (1865-1940)
Polish poet and writer.

Tolson, Melvin B. (1900-1966)
Black poet.

Toomer, Jean (1894-1967)
Black writer and poet.

Walker, Margaret (b. 1915)
Black poet.

Wasilewska, Wanda (1905-1964)
Polish author and political activist.

Wendroff, Zalman (1877-1971)
Pseudonym of Zalman Vendrovsky. Yiddish author and
journalist. In spite of his arrest in 1948 and subsequent
eight-year imprisonment, he supported Jewish and Yiddish
culture in the Soviet Union to his death.

White, Walter F. (1893-1955)
    Black author.

Whitfield, James M. (1830-1870)
    Black poet.

Williams, Jim
    Black poet.

Wright, Richard (1908-1960)
    Black writer.

Wygodski, Stanisław (b. 1907)
    Polish author.

Yeats, William Butler (1865-1939)
    Major Irish literary figure and poet. Nobel Prize winner in
    1923.

Żeromski, Stefan (1864-1925)
    Major Polish writer and patriot.

APPENDIX D
LIST OF CHINESE TRANSLATORS AND THEIR PENNAMES

An I-hsüan

安簪選

Chang Ch'i

張奇

Chang Lu-pei

張露𣱵

Chang Meng-lin

張蔓麟

Chao Ching-shen

趙景深

Chao Chung-ch'ien

趙仲謙

Ch'en Chen-kuang

陳珍广

Ch'en Ku

陳蝦

Ch'eng Tz'u-min

程次敏

Chi Sheng

吉生

Ch'iao Ts'eng-min

喬曾敏

Ching-wen

靜聞

Chung Ching-wen

鍾敬文

Ching Yüan

靜源

Cho Lin-hui

卓琳暉

Chou Chien-jen

周建人

Chou Shu-jen

周樹人

Penname:　Yüeh Wen

樂文

Chou Tso-jen

周作人

Penname:　Nan-ming

難明

Chou Tso-t'o

周佐佗

Chu T'i-jan

汪個然

149

150

Chu-yen

竹 衍

Chuang Shou-tz'u

莊 壽 慈

Chung Hsien-min

鍾 憲 民

Chung Yün

仲 云

Fang-ching

方 敬

Fei Pai

妃 白

Fu Ch'üan

馥 泉

Hai Kuan

海 觀

Hsi Tzu

席 犾

Hsia Ch'ing

夏 清

Hsieh Hsin-hui

謝 新 輝

Hsieh Wang-ying

謝 婉 瑩

    Penname: Ping-hsin

冰 心

Hsing Chen

惺 袗

Hsü Ping-ch'ang

徐 炳 昶

Hsü T'ien-hung

許 天 虹

Hu Chung-chih

胡 仲 持

Hu Yü-chih

胡 俞 之

    Penname: Hua Lu

化 魯

Hua K'an

華 侃

Huang Cho-han

黄 倬 漢

Huang I

黄 彝

Huang Sung-ch'i

黄 宋 綺

Huang Yüan

黄 源

Keng Shih-chih

耿 式 之

Ku Feng

谷 風

Ku Te-lung

顧 德 隆

Kuo Mo-jo

郭 沫 若

Li Chien-wu

李健吾

Li K'ai-hsien

李開先

Li Nien-p'ei

李念培

Ling-shan

凌山

Ling Tse-min

凌則民

P'ei Yüan-ying

裴远頴

P'ing Tsun-ping

(not available)

Pu Ch'eng-chung

卜咸中

Penname:　Sun Yung

孫用

Pu-chih

补之

Shen Tse-min

沈澤民

Shen Yen-ping

沈雁冰

Pennames:　Fen Chün

芬君

Hsi Chen

希真

Mao Tun

茅盾

Tung Fen

冬芬

Shih Chih-ts'un

施蟄存

Shih Yu-sung

施友松

Shou-ts'an

壽讚

Su Ch'in-sun

蘇芹蓀

Tai K'o-ch'ung

戴支崇

Penname:　Tu-heng

杜衡

T'ang Chen

湯真

T'ang Hsü-chih

唐旭之

Tseng Hsü-pai

曾虚白

Tu Ch'eng-ssu

杜承思

Tung Ch'iu-fang

董秋芳

Wang Heng

王衡

Penname: Lu-yen

魯彥

Wang Lu-yen

王魯彥

Wang Hsiao-yin

王小隱

Wang Hsin-ch'ing

王心清

Wang I

王易

Wang T'ung-chao

王統照

Penname: Wang Chien-san

王僉三

Wen-lan

文嵐

Ya-k'o, Ch'eng-ch'iu

亞支, 成秋

Yeh Ling-feng

葉靈鳳

Yin Yen

殷炎

Yü Huai-cheng

余懷證

GLOSSARY

Chang Chien
張謇

Chang T'ai-yen
章太炎

Chang Wei-tz'u
張慰慈

Cheng Chang
鄭昶

Ch'en Tu-hsiu
陳獨秀

Cheng Chen-to
鄭振鐸

cheng-li kuo-ku
整理國故

chi-an hui
輯安會

chia-hsiang
家鄉

Chiang Mon-lin
蔣夢麟

Chiao-yü yü chih-yeh
教育與職業

Chihli pai-hua pao
直隸白話報

ching-hsia
經匣

ching-shen
精神

Ching-yeh hsün-pao
競業旬報

Chou Yang
周揚

Chung-kuo hsin nü-chieh
中國新女界

Fan Chung-yün
樊仲雲

Fei Chien-chao
費鑑照

fu-huo
復活

fu-k'an
副刊

Hei-jen shih-hsüan
黑人詩選

153

ho-le i-ko lan-tsui
喝了一個爛醉

Hsi-kuo chin-shih hui-pien
西國近事彙編

Hsi Ti
西諦

Hsin-ch'ao
新潮

hsin tz'u-jan
新自然

hsin wen-hua
新文化

Hsin yüeh
新月

Hsin yüeh yüeh-k'an
新月月刊

Hsüeh-jen
雪人

hsün-shan
郇山

Hu Shih
胡適

hu-shih-ti
呼式忒

Huang Tsun-hsien
黃遵憲

Huang Yüan-yung
黃遠庸

hui-t'ang
會堂

jen-sheng kuan
人生觀

jen-tao chu-i che
人道主義者

jen ti wen-hsüeh
人的文學

jo-hsiao min-tsu
弱小民族

K'ang Yu-wei
康有為

k'e-hsüeh yü jen-sheng kuan
科學與人生觀

Ko Sui-ch'eng
葛綏成

Ku Chieh-kang
顧頡剛

ku-hsiang
故鄉

ku wei chin yung, yang wei chung yung
古為今用, 洋為中用

ku-wen
古文

kuan-hua
官話

Kuan-hua ho-sheng tzu-mu
官話合聲字母
kuo-yin tzu-mu
國音字母
kuo-yü
國語
kuo-yü ti wen-hsüeh, wen-hsüeh ti kuo-yü
國語的文學，文學的國語
Lao Nai-hsüan
勞乃宣
lao-t'ien-yeh
老天爺
li-shih ti wen-hsüeh chin-pu
歷史的文學進步
li-yü
俚語
Liang Ch'i-ch'ao
梁啓超
Lin Shu
林紓
Liu Pan-nung
劉半農
Lu Hsün
魯迅
Lu Kan-chang
(not available)

Min-li pao
民立報
min-tsu fu-hsing yün-tung
民族復興運動
min-tsu yün-tung
民族運動
ni chien-jen
你賤人
Nü-hsüeh pao
女學報
Pai-hua pao
白話報
p'ai-yu
排猶
pei-ya-p'o min-tsu
被壓迫民族
p'ing-hua
平話
p'ing-min ti wen-hsüeh
平民的文學
shang-ti
上帝
shen
神
Shen Yü
沈餘
Sheng Ch'eng
盛成

sheng-hui
生回

sheng-huo
生活

sheng-ming ti p'i-p'ing
生命的批評

Shih-pao
時報

Shih-shih hsin-pao
時事新報

shu
屬

ssu
寺

ssu-sheng yu ming-ah
死生由命啊

Su Man-shu
蘇曼殊

su wen-hsüeh
俗文學

Sun Fu-yüan
孫福怨

tao-mei-chia huo
倒眉家伙

Ting Ling
丁玲

tsai-sheng
再生

tsan-mei-shih
讚美詩

Ts'ao Ching-hua
曹靖華

Tsou T'ao-fen
鄒韜奮

tu-la
土拉

t'uan-p'ing
短評

t'uo-la
托拉

Wan-kuo kung-pao
萬國公報

Wang Chao
王照

Wang Che-fu
王哲甫

Wang Tso-liang
王佐良

wei-ta pu-tiao
尾大不掉

Wen-hsün hsün-k'an hsüan-yen
文學旬刊宣言

wen-hsüeh yen-chiu hui
文學研究會

wen-hua
文化

wen-i fu-hsing

文藝復興

wen-tzu k'e-ming

文字革命

Wu Ch'ing-yu

吳清友

Wusih pai-hua pao

無錫白話報

Yang Jui-ling

楊銳靈

Yao Hsiung

幼雄

Yü K'an

育幹

Yü Sung-hua

俞頌華

Yü Ta-fu

郁達夫

yu-t'ai li-pai-t'ang

猶太禮拜堂

Yü-wai hsiao-shuo chi

域外小説集

INDEX OF NAMES AND TERMS

MICHIGAN PAPERS IN CHINESE STUDIES

No. 2. *The Cultural Revolution: 1967 in Review,* four essays by Michel Oksenberg, Carl Riskin, Robert Scalapino, and Ezra Vogel.

No. 3. *Two Studies in Chinese Literature,* by Li Chi and Dale Johnson.

No. 4. *Early Communist China: Two Studies,* by Ronald Suleski and Daniel Bays.

No. 5. *The Chinese Economy, ca. 1870-1911,* by Albert Feuerwerker.

No. 8. *Two Twelfth Century Texts on Chinese Painting,* by Robert J. Maeda.

No. 9. *The Economy of Communist China, 1949-1969,* by Chu-yuan Cheng.

No. 10. *Educated Youth and the Cultural Revolution in China,* by Martin Singer.

No. 11. *Premodern China: A Bibliographical Introduction,* by Chun-shu Chang.

No. 12. *Two Studies on Ming History,* by Charles O. Hucker.

No. 13. *Nineteenth Century China: Five Imperialist Perspectives,* selected by Dilip Basu, edited by Rhoads Murphey.

No. 14. *Modern China, 1840-1972: An Introduction to Sources and Research Aids,* by Andrew J. Nathan.

No. 15. *Women in China: Studies in Social Change and Feminism,* edited by Marilyn B. Young.

No. 17. *China's Allocation of Fixed Capital Investment, 1952-1957,* by Chu-yuan Cheng.

No. 18. *Health, Conflict, and the Chinese Political System,* by David M. Lampton.

No. 19. *Chinese and Japanese Music-Dramas,* edited by J. I. Crump and William P. Malm.

No. 21. *Rebellion in Nineteenth-Century China,* by Albert Feuerwerker.

No. 22. *Between Two Plenums: China's Intraleadership Conflict, 1959-1962,* by Ellis Joffe.

No. 23. *"Proletarian Hegemony" in the Chinese Revolution and the Canton Commune of 1927,* by S. Bernard Thomas.

No. 24. *Chinese Communist Materials at the Bureau of Investigation Archives, Taiwan,* by Peter Donovan, Carl. E. Dorris, and Lawrence R. Sullivan.

MICHIGAN ABSTRACTS OF CHINESE AND
JAPANESE WORKS ON CHINESE HISTORY

No. 1. *The Ming Tribute Grain System*, by Hoshi Ayao, translated by Mark Elvin.

No. 2. *Commerce and Society in Sung China*, by Shiba Yoshinobu, translated by Mark Elvin.

No. 3. *Transport in Transition: The Evolution of Traditional Shipping in China*, translations by Andrew Watson.

No. 4. *Japanese Perspectives on China's Early Modernization: A Bibliographical Survey*, by K. H. Kim.

No. 5. *The Silk Industry in Ch'ing China*, by Shih Min-hsiung, translated by E-tu Zen Sun.

No. 6. *The Pawnshop in China*, by T. S. Whelan.

NONSERIES PUBLICATION

Index to the "Chan-kuo Ts'e," by Sharon Fidler and J. I. Crump. A companion volume to the *Chan-kuo Ts'e*, translated by J. I. Crump (Oxford: Clarendon Press, 1970).

Michigan Papers and Abstracts available from:

Center for Chinese Studies
The University of Michigan
Lane Hall (Publications)
Ann Arbor, Mi 48109 USA

Prepaid Orders Only
write for complete price listing